## DATE DUE

| | | | |
|---|---|---|---|
| MY 29 '97 | | | |
| OC 24 '97 | | | |
| DE 12 '97 | | | |
| RENEW | | | |
| MY 27 99 | | | |
| DE 11 00 | | | |
| NY 12 '93 | | | |
| | | | |
| | | | |
| | | | |
| | | | |
| | | | |
| | | | |
| | | | |
| | | | |
| | | | |
| | | | |

# CHOOSING THE
# PRESIDENT
## —1992—

CHOOSING THE

# PRESIDENT

## 1992

### THE LEAGUE OF WOMEN VOTERS
### OF
### CALIFORNIA EDUCATION FUND

★ ★ ★

**LYONS & BURFORD, PUBLISHERS**

*This work was prepared with the permission of the League of Women Voters Education Fund.*

*Printed in the United States of America*
*10 9 8 7 6 5 4 3 2 1*

Library of Congress Cataloging-in-Publication Data

Choosing the president—1992 / The League of Women Voters of California Education Fund.
p.    cm.
Includes bibliographical references  (p.    ) and index.
ISBN  1-55821-171-3.  —  ISBN  1-55821-169-1  (pbk.)
1. Presidents—United States—Election—1992.  I. League of Women Voters of California.   Education Fund.
JK526   1992b
324.973'0928—dc20  91-47912
CIP

# CONTENTS

| | | |
|---|---|---|
| *Acknowledgments* | | *vi* |
| **1** | On Choosing the President | *1* |
| **2** | The Political Framework: The Parties | *5* |
| **3** | The Political Framework: The Voters | *13* |
| **4** | The Preliminaries | *24* |
| **5** | Campaign Financing | *31* |
| **6** | Delegate Selection | *50* |
| **7** | The Convention | *62* |
| **8** | The General Election Campaign | *75* |
| **9** | The Election | *91* |
| | *Afterword* | *104* |
| | *Appendixes* | *106* |
| | *Bibliography* | *130* |
| | *Index* | *135* |

# ACKNOWLEDGMENTS

To give due credit to others in the production of a book is always a difficult task. It is particularly true in the case of *Choosing the President,* which has been published and republished during presidential election years. This edition revises past editions. The 1972 edition was principally the work of Mary Morgan, with the help of Daphne White. The research and major revisions in the 1976 edition were the work of Annette Kornblum, under the supervision of Beth Perkins, with rewriting done by Madelyn A. Bonsignore. The revisions for the 1980 edition were made by Sheri Lanoff, with the help of Karen Lebovich. The 1984 revisions were the work of Mary N. Stone, Marlene Cohn, and Patricia M. Hawkins, assisted by Marie Tessier and Matthew Freeman, under the supervision of Mary Stone. The 1992 edition was revised by Judith Hoefling, Trisha Garretson, Susan Heath, and Virginia Birdsall. Graphs were created by Kim Hellinge.

# 1

# ON CHOOSING THE PRESIDENT

The president of the United States is the most powerful elected official in the world. The United States Constitution, political realities, and historical precedents combine to give the president a position in the American system of government unmatched by that of executives in other democratic countries. Indeed, even executives in nondemocratic countries may not be as strong. They must give considerable attention to the possibility of overthrow, whereas presidents of the United States rest secure in the knowledge that their power is based upon consent.

Over the years, the powers of the president as outlined in the Constitution have been greatly expanded by many occupants of the office. The president has emerged as the chief political figure in the United States, despite the checks and balances established by the separation of powers and the federal system of government. With an election system that makes the executive branch politically independent of the other two branches of government and gives presidents *de facto* leadership of their political parties, our chief executives have usually won their battles with Congress and with the Supreme Court. Recent presidents have been aided by their large and expert staffs. Although power ebbs and flows among the three branches of government, the modern president plays a pivotal role.

Twentieth-century demands on government have further encouraged this trend. The president commands the large military forces of the nation and the major part of a vast civil bureaucracy. In addition, we expect the president to develop and advocate legislation in areas of national concern, to serve as a symbol of the nation united, and even to establish and maintain trends in national morals and mores. Historically the president has been the key figure in American foreign policy. However, since the 1930s the president has had an increasing influence in domestic policy as well. Whether negotiating an arms-control treaty, instituting new social programs, or formulating major economic policies, the president clearly affects the life of every person in the United States. The choosing of a president, then, is of great significance to every American.

Television broadcasts of national party conventions and candidate debates have drawn millions of people into the excitement of nominating and electing the president and vice president. Some watch these proceedings only as spectators. Others feel the personal involvement that comes from understanding and participating in the process.

An understanding of how political parties function and how they fit into the governmental structure is necessary in order to understand how a presidential candidate becomes a party's official nominee. It is helpful to know a few details about how the national political party conventions are organized and how they operate. In this multimedia age it is also important to be aware of campaign techniques, strategies, and costs. The Federal Election Campaign Act (FECA) of 1971 as amended has made significant changes in the funding of federal elections. Moreover, individuals need to understand all phases of the election process so that they can more clearly perceive how to be effective—how to have their voices heard in the choosing of the president.

A president is elected only once every four years, but the *process* of election never really stops; it simply moves from one phase to the next. The preliminaries extend from the presidential inauguration on January 20 to the next presidential election year.

During the years between presidential elections a future presidential contender attempts to build a strong and far-reaching record (either as an officeholder or as a spokesperson for a broad national constituency), to gain the attention of the media, to develop solid areas of political strength, and to secure political commitments and endorsements.

Before the primaries and national political conventions, contenders must decide whether to become candidates and, if so, in which states to concentrate their efforts. Delegates to the national conventions are selected during this period through either party caucuses or primaries, and candidates attempt to gain support from as many states as possible.

The days that each national convention is in session can be a time of high drama as candidates for president and vice president are finally nominated and party platforms are nailed down. Losing contenders at the convention may close ranks behind the winner, choose to sit out the election, or secede from their party and lead third-party or independent movements of their own. The presidential campaign extends from summer to election day in November, concluding in the election itself, the formalities of the results, and the inauguration.

The presidential election takes place within the context of a well-established political framework: a system of institutionalized political parties and a large and ever-changing electorate. Most presidential candidates are nominated by political parties; they campaign as partisans and are assisted to election by parties.

At every stage in the election process the voters are called upon to make choices. They assess the records of the various contenders, often express a preference in a precinct caucus or a primary, evaluate the convention choices, and vote on election day. Many citizens also campaign on behalf of their candidates in primary and election campaigns.

*Choosing the President* describes the political process for presidential elections, including the political parties, the voters, and the five phases of the election process. The appendixes offer supplemental facts and figures.

# 2

## THE POLITICAL FRAMEWORK: THE PARTIES

Every candidate for president since George Washington has run for office with the support of one of the two major parties of the period. In fact, supporting the election of a national executive was a main impetus behind the rise of national parties. Once they were established, they continued to shape the process by which presidents are chosen.

### The Role of the Parties[1]

Political parties perform a number of basic functions. Seen from the viewpoint of the voter, parties help clarify issues, relate candidates to these issues, and simplify the choices the citizen must make in elections. In addition, parties give some coherence to government and give the citizen a basis for judging that government and holding it accountable for its acts. Without parties, citizens would have to find their way with little assistance through a confusing maze of issues, candidates, and government actions. Seen from the viewpoint of political leaders, parties are the link among the three branches of the federal government and among local, state, and federal governments. Parties are also the means whereby party supporters are identified and mobilized behind candidates and programs. To use a familiar concept, parties are "brokers" that help to translate the wishes of people into government policy.

The U.S. Constitution predates the rise of political parties; the document, therefore, makes no mention of them. Although now regulated by federal and state law, parties have developed entirely as extraconstitutional bodies. As early as the 1790s, parties began to control the electoral college system and soon were exercising influence on all elections. Today, most federal and state officeholders, and many local ones as well, are chosen on a partisan basis. Despite this long history of party control of American politics, a popular belief in the desirability of being "nonpartisan" persists, based in part on an association of parties with "spoils" and corruption.

From the beginning, American politics has been dominated by two major parties. However, the constituencies of these parties have changed considerably over the years as some groups have moved from one party to another and new groups have been incorporated. The Democratic-Republicans of the Jefferson era were succeeded by the Democrats of Jackson's time, and that party continues today. The Federalists evolved into the Whigs, and the remnants of that group and new groups were incorporated into the Republican party under Lincoln. For the last hundred years, the two parties have stabilized as the Democratic and the Republican parties and have regularly contested national elections.

Traditionally, the United States has had a two-party system rather than a multiparty system because our electoral processes have fostered it. Since the mid to late 1960s, however, some political analysts have questioned whether the two major political parties effectively address the needs and wants of voters and appeal to virtually all segments of American society as they once did. In fact, the number of voters identifying themselves as independents has increased beginning with the 1968 election.[2]

Two-party politics has also been modified by other factors. Distrust and cynicism have enlarged the numbers of political nonparticipants, for example. Elections in the 1980s saw an accelerated rise in the number and type of extraparty, single-issue groups that played roles in state elections, in some congressional races, and in the presidential election itself. Such groups have demonstrated an ability to raise large amounts of campaign money and thus to have an impact on some election results.

There is some disagreement over the future of the American two-party system. Will the future bring a realignment[3] of constituents within the two major parties? Will it mean an entirely new party taking the place of either the Democratic or the Republican party? Or will it bring, more drastically, a breakdown into a multiparty system?

# Party Structure

Each major party organization has at least four, sometimes five, distinct geographical tiers. The precincts are the bottom layer. At the top stands the figure of the chair of the national committee.

The titular heads of the parties are the president and the defeated nominee of the other party, but their positions are of varying importance in party organization. Some presidential candidates, for example, have had little party influence during the four years following their defeat at the polls. In recent years, defeated Democratic party candidates have chosen not to play a visible role in party politics, thus leaving a void to be filled by potential presidential candidates and the chair of the Democratic National Committee.

Each tier of the party's organization is dependent on the layer below it. In addition, each tier, from precinct to national committee, has its special responsibility within its geographical area in the elections.

Following is an outline of the structure of the official organization of the two major political parties. The actual situation is far less tidy than this description implies, however. Aside from the national committee, neither party has a complete working organization at each level, except during election campaigns. Some precincts in some very large cities or even in some counties do not have a full organization for either major party.

Each of these political layers, including those not in the limelight during the nominating conventions, plays a vital role in choosing the nominees for, and in electing, the president and the vice president.

## THE PRECINCT

The precinct, an election district in a county, is the basic unit in the political structure where party workers begin their operations in political campaigns. Some cities also have wards that are composed of several precincts. Precincts across the country are headed by precinct captains or precinct leaders. (Other titles are also used.) Leaders may be chosen at caucuses, at direct primary elections, or in the general election, or they may be appointed by higher party officials. The precinct leader is the direct link between voters in the precinct and the professional political group. This leader is the party organization person who, through block workers and other aides, knows a great deal about the individual voters in the precinct and has substantial direct influence on them. Through this leader, the working members of the party at the precinct level may make their voices heard in the selection of delegates.

## THE COUNTY COMMITTEE

The county committee, the party tier just above the precinct (in larger cities, just above the ward or district) is a unit of major significance to the party machinery. The chairperson represents local precinct leaders on the state committee. Additionally, he or she is directly responsible for the efforts of precinct officials and local party leaders in getting out the vote on election day. The committee itself consists of precinct officials or alternates. The nation's 3,200-plus counties are important functioning political entities.

## THE STATE COMMITTEE

The state committee (or state central committee) forms the tier above the county committee. The authority and composition of state committees are usually specified in state law. They range in size from a handful of people to hundreds of members. Methods of selection differ widely from state to state. The chief function of state committees is to conduct campaigns through their officers and agents and to help in governing the party. They may also influence the choice of delegates to the national conventions, whatever the official selection process may be. In some cases the state committee still selects some delegates. When states have conventions to select delegates, the state committee wields great influence. Even in states that select delegates via the primary method, control of the state committee may be extremely important.

## THE NATIONAL COMMITTEE

The national committee is the top layer of party organization. This committee has representatives, at least one man and one woman, from each state and is of prime importance in the choosing of the president. The chair of the committee is a top-ranking professional politician. The powers and duties of the committee are dictated by the national convention.

"Kingpin of the national organization,"[4] the national committee chair is theoretically elected by the national committee but in practice is designated, immediately after the national convention, by the party's presidential candidate.

National committee members may be described as top politicians in their states. They are selected by the states in a variety of ways. Two of the most common ways are election by the state convention and election by the state's delegates to the national convention. In a number of states, committee members are elected by the voters in the primary, and some state committees appoint the national members. They are often wealthy, because membership on the national committee is costly in both time and money. Many national committee members are experts in law, business, and politics.

The national committee members may be the unquestioned statewide party leaders, or their power may emanate from a densely populated area in the state. They may be close aides of the party leaders, or they may be receiving rewards for generous contributions of money or for years of party service or distinction.

Apart from its internal structure, each party also has a Senate Campaign Committee and a Congressional Campaign Committee, selected in each new Congress at conferences of party members. These committees raise funds and help in the campaigns of candidates for the Senate and the House of Representatives.

# Other Political Groups

In addition to the regular party organizations in the United States, there are many auxiliary political groups outside the formal party structure that appeal to special segments of the party membership—the National Federation of Republican Women and the Young Democrats, for example. In addition, there are splinter groups or factions within the parties that may represent dissatisfaction with the leadership.

Other political groups or committees are mandated by law. The Federal Election Campaign Act, for example, requires that candidates for president who either receive more than $5,000 in contributions or spend more than $5,000 within a campaign cycle name a principal campaign committee through which all contributions to the candidate's campaign chest and all expenditures made in the candidate's name are reported to the Federal Election Commission. These committees are not part of the regular party structure but are official committees tied to the individual candidate.

## THIRD PARTIES AND INDEPENDENT CANDIDATES

In the history of the American presidency, hundreds of third-party candidates have sought the presidency, but only eight have won more than a million votes.[5] However, third or minor parties play an important role in American politics. These parties frequently form whenever the electorate is deeply divided over issues. In the past, for example, conflicts over slavery, economic reform, and integration were catalysts for the reemergence of third parties. The National Organization for Women (NOW), motivated by its belief that neither of the major parties will satisfactorily address women's issues, is considering forming a third party to run a presidential candidate in 1992.

The Republican party was once a third party; the Populist party attempted to replace the Democratic party in the 1890s; Theodore Roosevelt formed the "Bull Moose" party in the 1912 election; in 1924, the Progressives, led by Wisconsin Senator Robert La Follette, got 17 percent of the popular vote by addressing the issue of corporate domination.

In a few states there are third parties that are important at the state level but do not compete for national office; nonetheless, by forming coalitions they can wield considerable influence. In 1970 the Conservative party candidate, James L. Buckley, won the U.S. Senate race in New York.

In the modern political era only once has a third party, in a presidential election, come close to winning the 17 percent of the popular vote scored by La Follete in 1924. In 1968 the American

Independent party, led by Governor George Wallace of Alabama, won 9,906,473 popular votes or 13.5 percent of the total popular vote and 46 electoral votes.[6]

In 1976 former Minnesota Senator Eugene McCarthy ran for president as an independent, but he lacked the funds, the national constituency, and the campaign organization to mount a strong candidacy. In 1980 Illinois Congressman John Anderson failed to gain the Republican party nomination and then ran as an independent, winning 5,720,060 popular votes, placing him second, in popular votes, to Alabama Governor George Wallace as the most successful third-party or independent candidate for president in America's history.

## *Notes*

1. See V. O. Key, Jr., *Politics, Parties and Pressure Groups*, a classic work on American parties.
2. Richard A. Watson, *The Presidential Contest*, 3d ed., p. 99.
3. Realignment refers to lasting change in political behavior and party loyalties, generally in response to a stirring issue. Some political scientists believe that there have been five major realignments in American political history. In 1800, the issue was the power of the national government; in 1828, Jacksonianism; in 1860, slavery; in 1896, monetary policy and capitalism; in 1932, the Depression.
4. Key, *Politics, Parties and Pressure Groups*, p. 319.
5. *The World Almanac of U.S. Politics, 1991–1993 edition*, p. 23.
6. *Ibid.*, p. 25.

# 3

## THE POLITICAL FRAMEWORK: THE VOTERS

The efforts of the political parties and related political groups all point toward one objective—to bring to the polls on election day voters who will support their candidates. These voters, often referred to as the electorate, form the second major part of the political framework for American presidential elections.

## The Expansion of the Suffrage

The founding fathers did not have universal adult suffrage in mind as the power base of American government, even though they were opposed to arbitrary rule and had faith in popular sovereignty. In fact, in the earliest years of American democracy, with few exceptions, voting was the exclusive province of white males who owned property. By 1850, however, almost every state government had given all adult free males the right to vote. Gradually, through constitutional amendment and by federal and state law, the base of democracy has widened and the country has moved steadily in the direction of universal adult suffrage.

Since general voting qualifications were left to the states by the federal Constitution, constitutional amendments and federal statutes have often been employed to expand the electorate. States still set voting qualifications, but they may not deny the franchise because of race (Fifteenth Amendment) or sex (Nineteenth Amendment). The most recently ratified amendment, the twenty-sixth, provides that anyone 18 years of age or over may not be denied the vote on grounds of age. In addition, the Seventeenth Amendment allows the American people to vote directly for United States senators for the first time, the Twenty-third Amendment allows residents of the District of Columbia to vote for president, and the Twenty-fourth Amendment bans payment of a poll tax as a requirement for voting. These constitutional changes, together with early action by the states abolishing the initial property restrictions, have had the effect of legally extending the eligibility to vote to all citizens 18 years of age and over. (See Appendix C for text of amendments.)

# Voter Turnout And Procedural Problems

Being eligible to vote, of course, is not the same as voting. Despite enfranchisement of people on a group basis, many individuals still do not vote, although more people vote in presidential elections than in any other election. However, since the 1960 participation level of 62.8 percent, the turnout of the voting-age population has declined each election except for a very slight increase in 1980. (See graph on page 15.) (The decrease in voter turnout, beginning with the 1972 election, partially reflects the expansion of

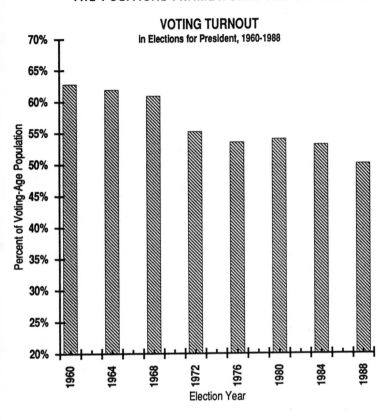

**VOTING TURNOUT**
In Elections for President, 1960-1988

*Source:* Mark S. Hoffman, ed., *The World Almanac and Book of Facts 1990* (New York: Pharos Books, 1990). Based on the Federal Election Commission: Commission for Study of American Electorate.

the voter enfranchisement to include citizens 18 to 21 years old.) In 1980, 54.0 percent of the voting-age population participated in the general election; in 1984, 53.1 percent; and in 1988, 50.1 percent.

Voting has never been compulsory in the United States as it is in some other countries. Therefore, turnout depends upon a wide range of motivating factors—voters' perceptions of candidates, issues, and parties; their sense of civic responsibility; their estimates of how effective government is; even their feeling of economic or physical safety. Still other factors keep people away from the polls—poor health, inadequate information about where and how to vote, local barriers to registration and voting, and transportation problems.

Apathy and dislike of politics in general or of the specific candidates in particular are also reflected in these voting trends. Some traditionally active voters may join the ranks of the younger, poorer, and less educated in turning away from the polls because they think their votes will not make much difference or because they do not care about a particular election.

In 1991, the Kettering Foundation published the results of a study by the Harwood Group on the state of America's democracy.[1] The study was concerned with the evidence that there is widespread public discontent about the American political system. Examples of this discontent are proposed term limitations, low voter turnout for elections, and issues placed on the ballot by citizens rather than being resolved in the legislatures by their representatives (particularly in California).

Citizens interviewed during the Harwood study were not apathetic toward voting, but rather expressed a frustration leading to anger and cynicism. These people believe two forces have corrupted the American political system: (1) lobbyists have replaced representatives as the primary political agents; and (2) campaign contributions seem to determine political outcomes more than voting. Consequently, many "people decide that voting really doesn't count anymore—so why bother."[2]

In the past, U.S. voter turnout has been adversely affected by procedural roadblocks that some citizens have encountered on the way to the voting booth. At the end of the nineteenth century, various kinds of requirements were established for those seeking to register to vote. They included lengthy residence requirements in states and precincts, registration deadlines far in advance of elections, poll taxes, long and complicated literacy tests, proof of good moral character, and frequent re-registration requirements. Although advocates of many of these processes claimed that such steps were necessary to prevent voting fraud, in fact, the impact was to depress electoral participation. The requirements constituted obstacles that voters had to overcome and affected mostly minorities and people with little education.

In recent years, many burdensome procedures have been abolished or at least eased. The Twenty-fourth Amendment in 1964 banned poll taxes in federal elections, and Supreme Court action outlawed such taxes in state elections. More recently, many states have improved their registration procedures. Twenty-eight states and the District of Columbia now have registration by mail, and three states have a form of election-day registration. North Dakota does not require voter registration of any sort.[3] Neighborhood and mobile registration sites are increasingly common, as are evening and Saturday hours for voter registration offices. Although the turnout rate has not increased nationwide, some observers maintain that it would be even lower had it not been for procedural improvements.

# The Voting Rights Act

The Voting Rights Act is a complex and detailed major law enacted by Congress in 1965 and reauthorized and expanded in 1970, 1975, and 1982. It was originally passed in response to demonstrations by black Americans protesting disenfranchisement. The act's basic intent is to ensure that racial and language minority citizens, wherever they live, have the same opportunity as other Americans to participate in the nation's political life.

The 1965 act forbids the use of literacy tests or other devices as qualifications for voting in any federal, state, local, general, or primary election. These tests had commonly been used to discriminate against racial and language minority citizens. The act also authorized the appointment of federal examiners to supervise electoral procedures in any state or county using such tests and where less than 50 percent of eligible voters were registered or had voted in 1964. Subsequently, this provision was extended to the 1968 election.

The Voting Rights Act of 1970 extended the 1965 act for five years, ensured that length-of-residence requirements would not prevent any citizen from voting in presidential elections, and provided uniform national rules for absentee registration and voting in presidential elections.

In 1975, the Voting Rights Act was extended for seven more years. Minority-language provisions were added to ensure that U.S. citizens are not deprived of the right to vote because they cannot read, write, or speak English. These citizens are defined in the act as people of Spanish heritage, Asian-Americans, American Indians, and Alaskan natives.

The 1982 act extends the law for 25 years. It also includes a 1973 Supreme Court decision *(White v. Regester)* that clarifies standards by which minority citizens can prove that their right to participate in the political process has been violated. Finally, blind, disabled, and illiterate persons are entitled to receive assistance at the polls by persons of their choice except the voter's employer or union representatives.

The Voting Rights Act has had a significant impact on voter registration and voting in the United States because the power of the federal government has been used to correct abuses at state and local levels. Consequently, several million blacks and other minority voters have registered to vote since the law went into effect.

In 1986, the U.S. Supreme Court handed down an important redistricting verdict as part of a test of the 1982 Voting Rights Act. The Court ruled *(Thornburg v. Gingles)* that any gerrymander of congressional district lines that purposely dilutes minority voting strength is illegal.[4]

Congress has considered measures to encourage greater voter turnout. Recently, the National Voter Registration Act of 1991, also known as the Motor Voter Bill, failed to pass. This would have allowed virtually all eligible citizens to apply to register at motor vehicle license bureaus, government agencies, or through the mail. Although members of the House and Senate have expressed concern about elections and the election process, they have so far deferred in most matters to state authority to run elections. Congress has, however, been more willing to act when basic voting rights are concerned. In addition to the Voting Rights Act, other laws passed by Congress have made absentee registration and voting easier for military personnel and their families and for American citizens living overseas.

# Voter Behavior

*Why* people vote as they do has always been of interest to scholars, to candidates, to the media, and to the people who conduct polls or manage campaigns. Analysis of voting statistics and public-opinion polls offer some tentative answers to perennial questions about voting patterns.[5]

Researchers on voting behavior point to three broad factors as being extremely important in influencing a voter's choice: partisan identification, issue preferences, and candidate preferences. Party affiliation has long been regarded as the major influence among the three, but in recent years issues have assumed more importance in elections. Also, voters' personal reactions to candidates, including assessment of leadership capabilities and responses to candidate images, are frequently significant.

Still, a political benchmark to keep in mind is that two-thirds of Americans are partisan—they identify with one of the two major parties. From 1980 through 1990, the number of Americans who identified themselves as Democrats ranged from 35 percent to 44 percent; Republicans ranged from 23 percent to 28 percent. In 1990, Americans identified themselves as 39 percent Democratic, 25 percent Republican, and 35 percent independent.[6] The party identification chart on page 20 gives such data from 1960 to 1990.

## PARTY IDENTIFICATION, 1960-1990

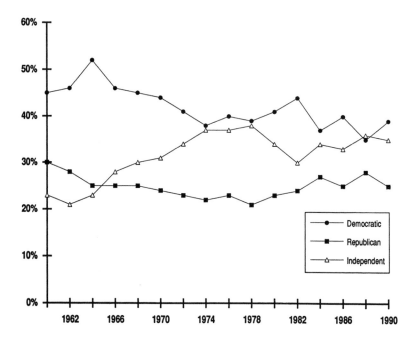

Source: Harold W. Stanley and Richard G. Niemi. *Vital Statistics on American Politics*, 3d ed. (Washington, D.C.: CQ Press, 1992), p. 158. Calculated by the editors from National Election Studies data (Center for Political Studies, University of Michigan, Ann Arbor, Michigan).

The percentage of independents has recently decreased somewhat after a spurt of growth from 1972 to 1984. Over a 40-year period, however, the proportion of independents has increased greatly from its low base of 22 percent in 1952. Although many believe that it is good to be an independent voter, independents actually dilute their voting effectiveness in many states because they have no voice in the process of nominating candidates through party primaries or caucuses. Studies show that the voter turnout record of independents falls below that of Democrats and Republicans.[7]

No matter what their political orientation, the overwhelming majority of voters seldom think of themselves in terms of "liberal" or "conservative." They respond instead to particular issues, a trend that has become increasingly important in influencing how the vote choice is made.

Another facet of voting behavior to be recognized is that groups sometimes tend to vote in certain ways. Blacks, who represent about 20 percent of the Democratic party's presidential electorate, tend to be the party's most loyal supporters and have on the whole backed Democratic candidates in the last seven presidential elections.[8] In 1984, 89 percent of blacks voted for Walter Mondale, and in 1988, 86 percent of blacks voted for Michael Dukakis.[9]

A recent trend is the increasing tendency for women to identify themselves as Democratic voters, reversing the 1950s trend when women tended to vote Republican. In the 1988 presidential election, women split their vote evenly between George Bush and Michael Dukakis (50 to 49 percent).[10]

The personal qualities of candidates also influence voting behavior heavily, sometimes overriding the pull of both parties and issues. President Eisenhower's popularity is considered a prime example. Voters also relate to politics on the basis of demographic factors such as education, ethnic background, occupation, income, and religion.

Democratic-Republican divisions in the voting public do not necessarily result in elections determined by those margins. Although less than one-third of the public is Republican, Republican candidates have won seven of the last ten presidential elections, partly because independents have tended to support the Republican presidential candidates in recent elections. Although President Johnson managed to capture 56 percent of the independent vote, President Eisenhower and President Nixon got even higher percentages in their victories. In 1980, 56 percent of independents voted for President Reagan, and in 1984, 63 percent did so. George Bush received 55 percent of the independent vote in 1988.[11]

Ticket splitting is yet another factor that is becoming more prevalent. (Ticket splitters vote for a president of one party and a member of Congress from another party, for example.) Voters may respond to state and local issues and candidates independently of presidential issues and candidates, or they may have strong emotional ties to a party at a local level but not at the national level.

Perhaps the most startling example of the ticket-splitting phenomenon occurred in 1972. For the first time in history, a president was elected with more than 60 percent of the popular vote without his party's gaining seats in the House and Senate or winning a majority in either congressional or gubernatorial elections. Despite the growing number of ticket splitters and independents, however, party identification is still believed to be a strong determinant of how a voter will cast a ballot.

Overall knowledge of voter behavior helps in predicting political trends and group voting patterns over a period of years, but it cannot be used reliably to forecast winners in every election or to predict the voting choices of an individual.

# *Notes*

1. See *Citizens and Politics: A View from Main Street America*, prepared for the Kettering Foundation by The Harwood Group.
2. *Ibid.*, p. v.
3. Office of California Secretary of State.
4. *The World Almanac of U.S. Politics, 1991-1993 edition*, pp. 15–16.
5. A number of studies include research on this subject and reach similar conclusions. Among the best known are *The American Voter* by Angus Campbell et al.; *Who Votes?* by Raymond Wolfinger and Steven Rosenstone; *Women and Politics* by Sandra Baxter and Marjorie Lansing; and *Voter's Choice*, by Gerald M. Pomper.

6. Harold W. Stanley and Richard G. Niemi, *Vital Statistics on American Politics*, 3d ed., p. 158. "Question: 'Generally speaking, do you consider yourself a Republican, a Democrat, an Independent, or what?' If Republican or Democrat: 'Would you call yourself a strong (R/D) or a not very strong (R/D)?' If independent or other: 'Do you think of yourself as closer to the Republican or Democratic party?'"
7. David B. Hill and Norman R. Luttbeg, *Trends in American Electoral Behavior*.
8. Joint Center for Political Studies.
9. Gerald M. Pomper et al. *The Election of 1988—Reports and Interpretations*, p. 134.
10. *Ibid.*, p. 122.
11. *Ibid.*, p. 133.

# 4

---

# THE PRELIMINARIES

---

T̲he political events that occur between presidential elections vary depending upon whether the persons involved are members of the in-party (the party that controls the presidency) or the out-party or -parties.[1] However, all parties and all prospective candidates have to do three essential things in this period: establish a record that will make candidacy possible (although this usually begins years before); develop a power base from which a candidacy can be launched; and devise a strategy to obtain the convention delegate support necessary to win the nomination.

## In-Party Preliminaries

The decisions of all prospective candidates in the in-party are heavily affected by the fact that a member of their party is in the White House. Historically, incumbent presidents have been hard to defeat in an election, and it has been considered nearly impossible to wrest the nomination away from them if they want it. (The Twenty-second Amendment, ratified in 1951, forbids a president from being elected to office more than two times.) For 1992, it is generally understood that George Bush may have the Republican nomination if he is available and wants to run. Looking back, however, it is generally conceded that Eugene McCarthy's strong showing in the 1968 New Hampshire Democratic primary greatly influenced President Lyndon Johnson's decision not to seek his party's nomination. In 1976, Ronald Reagan's challenge to President Gerald Ford's Republican candidacy also upset historical precedent. Many observers thought that Ford's apparent vulnerability could be attributed to his being the first nonelected (as either president or vice president) president in our history. Appointed to the vice presidency before becoming president, he had never run for either office. Although Reagan's strategy was unsuccessful at the time, it set the stage for his nomination four years later and his eventual victory over President Jimmy Carter in 1980.

Sitting presidents have only rarely been denied renomination when they sought it. In fact, those few who were not renominated by their parties had succeeded to the top slot from the vice presidency upon the death of the president. The presidents rejected for their party's renomination were John Tyler in 1844, Millard Fillmore in 1852, Andrew Johnson in 1868, and Chester A. Arthur in 1884.

Whether a president seeks reelection or not, however, it is his presidential record that the in-party will carry into the next campaign. From a political standpoint a president must build a legislative, executive, and diplomatic record that will stand his party in good stead. Policy promises must be kept and political commitments fulfilled. Especially important to the in-party is the midterm election in which all House seats and a third of the Senate seats are filled. Historically, the in-party loses congressional seats in the midterm election. If losses are significant, they will be interpreted as a repudiation of the president and his policies, so he has to work to minimize losses and maintain party morale. As the presidential election approaches, he must pay even more attention to the political impact of his actions.

The presidency is the best power base from which to launch a candidacy. If the incumbent does not seek reelection, other candidates must use whatever sources of strength they have. In modern times, the vice presidency seems to be a good spot for gaining a nomination, but not a particularly good one for winning an election. A vice president has the advantage of executive experience, media attention, and presidential support, but on the other hand he is stuck with the presidential record for better or worse. Since experience has shown that disunity is fatal, he must stand with the record and perhaps fall with it, as Vice President Hubert Humphrey did in 1968. Governors, senators, and perhaps a former candidate may also decide to run if the president steps down.

If a president decides to seek another term, his strategy during the preliminary period will be simple: maintain party harmony and make sure he controls enough party machinery to ensure that the party convention will be a mere formality, renominating him by acclamation and stoutly defending his policies. In the past, the decision of whether to dump an incumbent vice president has come at a later stage. Vice President Nelson A. Rockefeller's vow early in the 1976 race not to run with President Ford may have set a new pattern.

If a president steps down, other contenders will have many decisions to make: when to announce their candidacy, how heavily to lean on the president in winning delegates, how to use presidential primaries, and so forth. In 1968, Senator Robert F. Kennedy tried to win nomination through the primary route; Senator Eugene McCarthy mounted an extensive grass-roots campaign effort; Vice President Humphrey worked behind the scenes with presidential support. By and large, in-party strategies are determined by circumstances, the most important of which is the position taken by the incumbent president.

# Out-Party Preliminaries

Presidential contenders in the out-party (or parties) are in a position quite different from that of their in-party counterparts and may even have an advantage if the president does not seek reelection. Since they have not been responsible for broad legislative programs, executive actions, or diplomatic initiatives, they can criticize presidential efforts in all areas. Even if the out-party controls the Congress, an individual aspirant cannot be held to account because the out-party does not usually develop a broad legislative program of its own, responding instead to presidential actions.

To be sure, a presidential hopeful must build a creditable *individual* record. A governor or a mayor who is a contender will, of course, have a public record. But records can be, and often are, more in the nature of promises than accomplishments.

To build a record at all, an out-party aspirant needs a power base. Although candidacies are sometimes launched from appointive positions (Eisenhower in 1952) or private law practice (former Vice President Mondale in 1984), an elective office is considered best. A party's titular leader (usually the most recent losing presidential candidate) will probably try to gain such a position as soon as possible. After 1968, Humphrey sought and won his old Senate seat from Minnesota at the first opportunity; after 1972, George McGovern concentrated on retaining his Senate seat from South Dakota.

In recent years, because of the power and prestige of the position and the modern importance of international affairs, the Senate, rather than state or local government, has been a good place for individuals with presidential ambitions. In 1976, however, candidates from many different arenas emerged. Of the eleven announced Democratic presidential contenders at the start of the campaign season, only four were senators, and a fifth was a former senator. Of the six other candidates, two were former governors, two were sitting governors, one was a U.S. representative, and one was a former Democratic vice presidential nominee.

Early in the 1988 campaign, Senator Gary Hart, the 1984 Democratic runner-up, was the leading preference among Democratic voters, followed by the Reverend Jesse Jackson. Although many favored New York Governor Mario Cuomo, he refused to run. However, Gary Hart withdrew after public attention focused on indiscretions in his private life, and his campaign was thoroughly discredited. Additionally, Delaware Senator Joseph Biden announced his candidacy only to be discredited after he was discovered to have plagiarized speeches and exaggerated his academic accomplishments. Cuomo's decision not to run allowed Massachusetts Governor Michael Dukakis to attract the Northeast Democratic support.

Preceding the Democratic convention, Dukakis selected as his running mate Senator Lloyd Bentsen of Texas, a moderate who would broaden the party's appeal toward the center and the right wing of the electorate. This move angered Jackson and his supporters as well as the left wing of the party.

In the earliest stages of the preliminaries, contenders try to build a favorable image in the party and in the country by making frequent public speeches and appearances at party functions. If prospects seem bright and financial backing emerges, this period of active "noncandidacy" will be followed by a formal announcement. The Federal Election Campaign Act discourages the formerly common practice of front-runners waiting until the last minute to announce their entry into the race. Limits on the size of campaign contributions mean that those who start raising money early have an advantage.

In the past, some contenders did not engage in preliminary campaigning at all but waited to be "drafted." These drafts were rarely genuine; rather, they were matters of strategy.[2] The recent proliferation in the number of primaries, straw votes, and caucuses makes the possibility of draft candidates unlikely.

Although some contenders use a middle-of-the-road appeal to broaden their base of support, others seek backing from particular special-interest groups. Usually there are only shades of differences between the hopefuls. In 1984 and 1988, Democratic candidates were mostly united in their opposition to the Republican administration's stands on social issues, the economy, defense spending, and the environment. In such circumstances, potential convention delegates would need to evaluate a candidate's potential to defeat the in-party rather than base a decision on ideological grounds.

Each contender must make a political decision whether to make a vigorous attack on the presidential record during the campaign. This choice is usually dictated by a contender's past record in this regard and by the current popularity of the incumbent. When a president's popularity ebbs, contenders are more inclined to play on antigovernment themes, as was the case in the 1976 and 1980 contests.

The final strategy decision centers on how to build delegate strength for the nominating convention. At this point, some of the earlier hopefuls will have withdrawn because they failed to get enough money or other support, and the field will be left to those with the most serious chances of success.

# The Media in the Preliminaries

The mass media, particularly television and the national newspapers and magazines, play important roles in the preliminary stage of presidential elections. They can virtually create a frontrunner by giving exposure or by declaring that the candidate is the front-runner. If they do not take a candidate seriously, it will be much harder for the contender to raise money and capture early delegate commitments. Obviously, a president who is a candidate has great advantages in media access. The president is news and gets coverage accordingly, and it seems impossible to nullify this built-in advantage. In recent years the out-party has tried (with only limited success) to get air time to reply to broadcast presidential statements of a partisan flavor. The networks do provide the opposition party with prime time to respond to the incumbent president's State of the Union address.

Charges of bias in the media are common and come from all sides. One of Vice President Agnew's first "official" acts was to denounce the media for their handling of President Nixon's program. Governor Wallace regularly complained that the media distorted his views.

During the 1972 campaign, Senator Edmund Muskie of Maine bitterly protested the way the press treated him; after his famous "emotional" scene outside the offices of the *Manchester Union Leader* newspaper, some political commentators who covered the campaign say Muskie never regained his stature as a credible candidate. On the other hand, a member of the 1976 Carter staff argued that Carter's *unfavorable* press coverage meant that he was finally being taken seriously.

Representative Shirley Chisholm, the first black woman to seek the presidential nomination, was never really taken seriously by the press. The political clout she developed during the 1972 campaign was surprising to most political commentators, yet most members of the press corps did not mention that she might pose a threat to other better-known liberal candidates.

Even incumbents are sensitive to the make-or-break powers of the media in the early stages of campaigning, when most of the jockeying for support goes on. In early 1976, President Ford seemed to feel he was "under the gun" from the press. According to president-watcher David Broder of the *Washington Post,* Ford responded by striking a "defiant" pose and staunchly defending some of his more controversial policies.

Early in the 1992 campaign, Democratic contenders and Republican President Bush alike began the traditional rounds of appearances before key groups. Such appearances are designed not only to appeal to particular interests but also to draw the attention of the media to campaign strategies and policy statements.

## Notes

1. The books by Theodore H. White on the making of the president offer some of the best material available on the preliminary period. Also see White's *America in Search of Itself.*
2. See Walter Johnson, *How We Drafted Adlai Stevenson.*

# 5

---

# CAMPAIGN FINANCING

---

When politicians say that "money is the mother's milk of politics," they are speaking the truth. Campaigns and elections are expensive, and costs have escalated greatly. Money is essential to political activity, whether we like it or not.

Presidential candidates need money to pay for television and radio time, air travel, computers and consultants to do polling, and direct mail to solicit voter support. In addition, there are the costs of operating telephone networks to communicate with voters as well as staff services and office costs associated with campaign activities. In an electronic age, presidential candidates are in a more competitive position if they have at least some access to all these capacities, and they are handicapped if they do not.

Presidential campaign spending has increased significantly in recent years. Campaign finance expert Herbert Alexander notes that in 1968, presidential campaign spending totaled $91 million. In 1972 this total jumped to $137.8 million, and by 1976 (the first year in which the total included independent expenditures made on behalf of candidates) spending reached $159.7 million. In 1980 the bottom line was $275 million; in 1984 it was $325 million; and in 1988 the cost of campaigning totaled approximately $500 million. Although these figures may seem high, Alexander maintains that they are relative when compared to the annual advertising budgets of commercial advertisers.[1]

"Money has attracted special notice in politics because of its easy conversion to diverse political uses, and because some people have a lot more of it than others," states campaign analyst Alexander Heard.[2] As we shall see, the intense interest in the financial aspect of political campaigns led to a decade of campaign finance laws during the 1970s, reforms that, in turn, led to the growth of what Herbert Alexander refers to as an "underground political economy" during the 1980s.[3]

# The 1971 Federal Election Campaign Act

The Federal Election Campaign Act (FECA) of 1971 was the first major overhaul of federal campaign legislation since the Federal Corrupt Practices Act of 1925. The 1971 act, as it applied to presidential or vice presidential candidates, limited contributions that the candidate could make to his or her own campaign to a maximum of $50,000. This restriction is applied to the candidate or members of his immediate family. It also established a spending limit for media advertising in presidential campaigns, a provision that was repealed in 1974. It specified limited spending per voter in presidential campaigns before the nominating convention.

FECA also provided for disclosure of contributions and expenditures and required the establishment of political committees for organizations that anticipated spending in excess of $1,000. It provided that enforcement of the act would be by the Clerk of the House and the Secretary of the Senate for congressional candidates and by the Comptroller General for presidential candidates.

The 1971 act also provided that radio and television broadcasters could charge political candidates only the lowest unit cost for the same advertising time as might be available to commercial advertisers. This lowest unit rule still applies, but only in the immediate preelection periods and then only to cheaper, preemptible time. (Most candidates want to be certain that their commercials will air; consequently they must purchase the more expensive non-preemptible or "fixed" time.)

FECA changed existing federal prohibitions on direct corporate and labor union contributions to campaigns by providing that such prohibitions did not forbid the establishment, administration, and solicitation of voluntary contributions to separate, segregated funds to be used for political purposes by labor unions and by corporations.

At the same time, Congress also amended the tax laws, under the Revenue Act of 1971, to establish the Presidential Election Campaign Fund. This provision allows taxpayers to contribute to the Presidential Campaign Fund through a $1 checkoff on their federal income tax forms ($2 for joint returns) without increasing their tax liability. Although close to 30 percent of taxpayers availed themselves of this opportunity in 1980, throughout the decade the percentage declined steadily, so much so that the solvency of the fund has come into question, and experts warn that the fund could be bankrupt by 1996.[4]

FECA also established a formula for distributing the presidential campaign funds raised through the tax checkoff to both major party candidates and minor and new party candidates. The 1971 act forbade major party candidates who chose public financing from accepting private contributions.

# The 1974 Amendments

Public disclosures during the Watergate investigations of illegal and "laundered" cash contributions from corporations and wealthy individuals to the 1972 Nixon reelection campaign committee shocked citizens and lawmakers alike. The public reporting requirements of the 1971 act *did not* prevent these very large amounts from being donated to campaign coffers in 1972, but they *did* allow citizens to know for the first time exactly who the donors were and how much they had given to whom.

To prevent further abuses Congress tightened FECA in 1974. Among other provisions, the 1974 amendments:

- Established a six-member, bipartisan Federal Election Commission (FEC) to be staffed by two commissioners appointed by the president, two by the Speaker of the House, and two by the president pro tempore of the Senate;
- Set individual contribution limits of $1,000 per candidate for each primary, general, or runoff election, and a total contribution limit of $25,000 per individual to all federal candidates, per year;
- Limited contributions from political committees and national or state party committees to $5,000 per candidate for each election;
- Set a limit of $1,000 for expenditures on behalf of a candidate made totally independent of the candidate;
- Established a $10 million total spending limit for each qualified major party candidate in a presidential primary race (with per state limits), based on voting-age population, and a $20 million limit for total spending for each nominee in the general election; these sums are pegged to the consumer price index and in 1988 were just over $23 million for the primary and $46 million for the general election;
- Gave federal funds of $2 million (since raised to $3 million and augmented each election according to the consumer price index—in 1988 totaling over $9 million) to each major political party to cover the costs of the national nominating conventions;

- Set up a system of public matching funds for presidential candidates in primary elections to take effect after the candidate reached a threshold of $100,000, raised in amounts of at least $5,000 per state, in 20 or more states, through individual contributions of $250 or less;
- Required candidates to establish a principal committee through which all their contributions and expenditures would be funneled and reported, and also required them to file detailed reports with the FEC;
- Permitted labor unions, government contractors, and corporations to establish segregated funds for political purposes only.

# Buckley v. Valeo

Within days after the 1974 act was passed, it was challenged in federal court by an ideologically mixed coalition including independent presidential candidate Eugene McCarthy, Conservative Republican Senator James Buckley, and General Motors heir and political philanthropist Stewart Mott. In January 1976, the Supreme Court issued a landmark decision in *Buckley v. Valeo* in which it tried to balance First Amendment rights against the interests of Congress and the public in reforming the campaign process. Basically, the Court upheld contribution limits and overturned expenditure limits. It outlawed both the limitation on independent expenditures and the limitation on candidates' expenditures on their own behalf as unconstitutional restrictions on the First Amendment rights of political expression.

The Court left in place, however, the overall personal candidate expenditure limits for candidates who accept public funds, ruling that Congress has the right to attach that condition to the use of public money. Further, it ruled that independent expenditures could not be made in collusion or in coordination with a candidate. These expenditures must be truly independent and spent by an individual or an organization without reference to any campaign or candidate consultation.

The Court upheld the overall limitations on contributions by both individuals and groups to campaign committees, stating that such limitations are acceptable under the Constitution because they serve to dilute the influence of large contributors and prevent undue influence on federal elections.

All the disclosure requirements were upheld by the Court, as were the public funding methods. Also left intact was the *concept* of a bipartisan commission to regulate the campaign finance law. However, the Court ruled that, under the constitutional concept of separation of powers, the president has the sole power to appoint the members of the commission, with the advice and consent of the Senate. This decision struck down the system whereby one-third of the commissioners was chosen by the president, one-third by the Speaker of the House, and one-third by the president pro tempore of the Senate, as the 1974 law had provided.

The Court gave Congress 30 days (later extended to 50 days) to reconstitute the FEC, but Congress was unable to act within that time. In March 1976, therefore, the FEC lost its ability to certify payments of matching funds, causing great concern among candidates during the 1976 primary period. It was not until May of that year that Congress was able to pass a revised law, restructuring the FEC and otherwise making the necessary amendments. After signing it, President Ford then delayed appointing the commissioners for another several days, in effect holding up matching money for contenders in the Michigan and Maryland primaries.

# The 1976 Amendments

The 1976 amendments to the Federal Election Campaign Act:

- Set a limit of $5,000 per year for individual contributions to political action committees (PACs) and provided that individuals could not give more that $20,000 per year to the national committee of a political party;

- Limited multicandidate committees[5] to giving no more that $15,000 a year to the national committee of a political party;
- Retained the 1974 contribution limit of $5,000 per election, per candidate, from a multicandidate committee;
- Set spending limits of $50,000 of their own or their family's money for presidential candidates who received public funds; and
- Established an independent Federal Election Commission, as the Supreme Court had required. The commission consists of six members, each appointed by the president and confirmed by the Senate, with no more than three from one political party. Also included on the panel are two nonvoting members: the Secretary of the Senate and the Clerk of the House.

In a significant action, the 1976 law restricted multiple corporate and union PACs from the same parent entity by providing that all PACs established by a company or by a union would be treated as a single committee for contribution purposes and that no PAC, whether union or corporate, could give more that $5,000 per candidate per election. Further, corporations, unions, and membership organizations were restricted from seeking contributions outside their purview. Companies could solicit contributions only from stockholders, executive and administrative staff, and families. Unions could solicit contributions only from their members and families. But communications from these separate segregated funds to the general public for the purpose of soliciting contributions were prohibited.

The 1976 amendments also strengthened the enforcement provisions of the Federal Election Commission. Unions, corporations, and membership organizations were required to disclose expenditures of more that $2,000 per election used to communicate to their stockholders or members concerning the election or defeat of a federal candidate.

# The 1979 Amendments

Following the 1976 election, and widespread complaints by parties and candidates about the burden of campaign record-keeping requirements, several changes were made in the law in 1979 to ease the process of compliance with FECA. The amendments:

- Raised the reporting requirement for federal candidates to a threshold of $5,000 in receipts or expenditures;
- Permitted local party organizations to avoid reporting certain voluntary activities valued at less that $5,000 (get-out-the-vote drives, voter registration drives, etc.);
- Permitted individuals to spend up to $1,000 on behalf of a candidate in providing voluntary services (use of a home for a meeting, food, travel, etc.) without these being considered contributions to the candidate;
- Required that the name of the candidate appear in all campaign committee titles;
- Required frequent reports to the FEC of the names of donors and amounts of donations of $200 or more (instead of the original $100 requirement);
- Required the reporting of independent expenditures of $250 or more (instead of the original $100 requirement);
- Strengthened the role of political parties by allowing them to conduct registration or get-out-the-vote drives without limit and to buy promotional products such as bumper stickers, brochures, and buttons without limit; and
- Allowed the allocation of $3 million in federal funds for the Democratic and Republican nominating conventions rather than the previous $2 million.

# Political Action Committees

Since the passage of FECA in the early 1970s, campaign spending patterns have been greatly affected by the growth in importance of PACs.[6] PACs exist to raise and spend campaign money. With strict federal restrictions on corporate, union, and individual contributions to campaigns, PACs have come to be a commonly used and relatively unencumbered way to raise and make political contributions.

PACs can refer to two types of noncandidate, nonparty political committees under the meaning of FECA (the term is not mentioned in the law). One refers to "separate, segregated funds"—political committees established by and affiliated with corporations, labor unions, trade membership organizations, cooperatives, or corporations without capital stock. The other refers to "nonconnected" political committees.

The separate, segregated fund type of PAC developed because of the federal prohibition on direct corporate, national bank, and union contributions to candidates for federal office. FECA made possible a means for separate political committees, organized by and tied to such institutions, to solicit and disburse voluntary contributions to candidates. Such PACs are restricted to communicating with their management, members, and families, and they may not make solicitations directed at the general public. Such affiliated PACs have the advantage of having their administrative and fundraising costs borne by the corporation, union, or membership association. About 75 percent of all PACs are of this separate, segregated fund type—that is, tied to the parent entity and accountable to it.

The second type of PAC—perhaps the one more commonly thought of—is the nonconnected political committee. These are independent committees usually organized by groups interested in one specific issue, whose purpose is to raise and spend money for campaign purposes. Such independent or nonconnected PACs are not bound by the restrictions that bind separate, segregated fund PACs when it comes to communications and fundraising. Nonconnected PACs can raise funds from the public (most do so by direct mail). They lack the advantage, however, of a parent organization to bear administrative and fund-raising costs.

Both kinds of committees can benefit from qualifying under federal law as multicandidate committees. In doing so, they increase their contribution limit to $5,000 per election per federal candidate ("persons" are restricted to $1,000).[7] To qualify as a multicandidate committee, a PAC must be registered with the Federal Election Commission for six months, receive contributions from more than 50 persons, and make contributions to five or more federal candidates.

A $1,000 contribution limit applies to persons or to organizations and groups unless the organization qualifies as a multicandidate committee. As a result, there is a five-to-one contribution-making advantage for multicandidate committees, an advantage that experts see as significant to the growth of PACs over the years. Since individuals cannot qualify as such a committee, they are restricted to a $1,000 contribution limit.

Who cares? Why is it important to know about PACs? A look at their growth and impact on campaign spending over time tells the story, and that story points to PACs as major funders of modern-day campaigns. In 1975 there were 608 PACs registered with the FEC. By the end of 1988 there were 4,268. (See graph on page 41 for an overview.)

Observers look not only at the growth in numbers of PACs but also at the growth in their receipts and contribution levels. There has been a sharp rise in the *amount* of campaign dollars accounted for by PAC activity, compared with the base level in the early 1970s. In 1980, PAC contributions to congressional candidates totaled $55.2 million and in 1988 had increased to a total of $151.3 million, whereas in 1972 the figure was an estimated $8.5 million.[8]

As for direct PAC contributions to presidential candidates, the numbers are relatively insignificant. This is because PAC contributions to primary election candidates cannot qualify for federal matching funds, and candidates in the general election operate under total public financing.

What the discussion thus far does not reflect is the role played by independent expenditures by PACs—or by individuals, for that matter—in presidential campaigns. Under the law, groups or individuals can spend unlimited dollars to support or oppose federal

**PAC GROWTH**

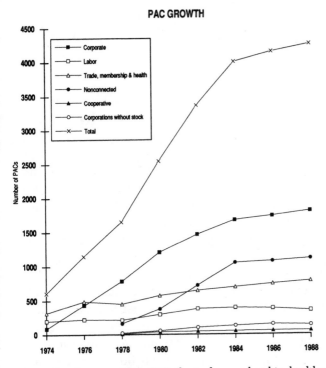

Note: For the years 1974–1976, the trade, membership, health category includes all PACs except corporate and labor. Nonconnected PACs do not have a sponsoring organization.

Sources: Michael Nelson, ed. *Congressional Quarterly's Guide to the Presidency.* (Congressional Quarterly Inc., Washington, D.C., 1989) p. 197 and Harold W. Stanley and Richard G. Niemi. *Vital Statistics on American Politics.* 2nd edition. (CQ Press, Washington, D.C., 1990) p. 160

candidates. The expenditures must be truly independent of a candidate's campaign; no collusion, even tacit, can exist.

Through the years there has been significant growth in the amount of money spent independently. In the 1976 presidential campaign, the first conducted under FECA, independent expenditures totaled $1.6 million. In 1980, $13.4 million was spent independently to support or oppose presidential candidates. By 1984 total independent expenditures in the presidential election reached $17.4 million, but the FEC reported that they fell approximately 19 percent to $14.1 million in 1988.[9]

# Effects of the Federal Election Campaign Act

The new method of financing our presidential campaigns has altered our election system in fundamental ways. From the initial decision to accept federal funding to the consequences and new strategies for meeting federal requirements to the development of adaptations to evade the requirements, presidential elections have evolved significantly since the passage of the Federal Election Campaign Act of 1971 and its amendments.

First of all, under FECA, presidential candidates must make the important initial decision of whether or not to accept federal funding and the expenditure limits that accompany it. All major candidates except John Connally in 1980 have accepted this funding, although a few others, including Ronald Reagan in 1980 and Marion G. (Pat) Robertson in 1988, considered refusing.

Second, the matching fund requirement for presidential primaries means that each presidential contender must set up functioning committees in 20 or more states at the outset of a campaign and receive numerous contributions of $250 or less. Some changes stemming from this include:

- Special advantages in fund-raising for presidential candidates with either national stature, e.g., George Bush running from his position as vice president in 1988, or access to lucrative fund-raising constituencies, such as Pat Robertson and Michael Dukakis, with widespread support in 1988 from the fundamentalist Christian community and Greek Americans, respectively;[10]

- A longer season for fund-raising, and thereby for campaigning;
- Latecomers being discouraged from entering the race;
- Candidates' strategies being altered in an attempt to meet and exploit the requirements (these changes include an increased reliance on both direct-mail solicitation in order to receive large numbers of small donations and front-loading—that is, raising and spending money wisely early in the campaign to achieve credibility and momentum, as Jimmy Carter's financially well-managed campaign did in 1976); and
- Awards of matching funds to only those candidates who received 10 percent or more of the vote in at least one of their two preceding primaries, which raises a dilemma of risking the loss of matching funds or the loss of potential delegates.

Finally, in the years since FECA took effect, presidential candidates and other political activists have created and implemented numerous strategies for evading the federal requirements that limit political contributions and expenditures. Campaign finance expert Herbert Alexander refers to this as a growing "underground political economy,"[11] and he divides the strategies into two groups: those that adapt FECA-regulated funding in an attempt to circumvent the intent of the law and those that escape FECA regulations altogether.[12]

Examples of circumvention techniques include:

- *Presidential PACs.* Created by prospective presidential candidates to finance their initial travel and support-gathering activities, these PACs ostensibly raise and spend money to promote a variety of political campaigns. In reality, however, most of these funds remain with the prospective candidate who organized the PAC, and they are not subject to the expenditure limits that apply to declared candidates seeking federal matching funds.

- *Independent expenditures.* As defined earlier, these are the unlimited dollars that groups or individuals can spend to support or oppose candidates. They must be truly independent of a candidate's campaign; no collusion, even tacit, can exist. Although the proliferation of PACs is seen by some as a positive sign of political participation by the many individuals who contribute to them, the dramatic increase in the number of PACs is also a source of controversy, attributable mainly to their use of these independent expenditures. Concerns about independent expenditures include three key questions:
- **1.** *Accountability.* Which PAC paid for an independent campaign and who are its constituents?
- **2.** *Use of the term "independent."* Is an expenditure truly independent? Many campaign experts feel that all too often it is not.
- **3.** *Political equality.* Does this ability to use independent expenditures benefit candidates equally, and will this method of financing increase the campaign impact of a given presidential candidate who has extensive independent expenditures made on his behalf?

These concerns are based on the patterns established in 1980, in which independent PAC expenditures on behalf of Ronald Reagan—$12.2 million—dwarfed the $46,000 spent on behalf of Jimmy Carter, a trend that was repeated again in 1984 and 1988 using the following techniques:

- *Bundling.* This is a technique in which individuals and PACs donate the maximum legal amount to a candidate's campaign fund and then contribute more money to an intermediary who will in turn channel that money to the same candidate.
- *Exploiting the compliance loophole.* Complying with FEC regulations has become so costly that the agency allows

candidates to exempt this expense from the spending limits; candidates may exploit this loophole by overstating such costs.

- *Evading state expenditure limits in the primaries.* Candidates have become very creative in this regard. For example, in order not to exceed spending limits in the crucial New Hampshire primary, candidates allocate many expenses to neighboring Massachusetts in the days preceding the New Hampshire vote.

Money that can be legally spent outside the prohibitions and requirements of FECA is known as "soft money." To show the extent to which it is used, one need only look at figures from the 1988 election. Although legally each major-party presidential campaign was allowed to spend about $54 million ($46 million from public funds, $8.3 million from their party's funds), each actually raised and spent over $100 million, and according to Congressional Quarterly, Inc., soft money accounted for most of the difference.[13]

So-called soft money is typically contributed directly by donors (including corporate and union treasuries, which are prohibited from contributing under federal law but are permitted to do so in many states) to state parties. These state parties can in turn spend unlimited undisclosed amounts to finance state and local party activities such as voter registration and turnout drives, as well as for purchasing such items as bumper stickers and brochures. Although ostensibly these expenditures affect only state and local elections, in reality this money inevitably influences presidential elections as well. Also, money spent in this way relieves the presidential campaign committee of the burden of spending its funds for such purposes and permits the campaign to allocate those resources to other uses.

Soft money can take on other forms as well. For example, unlimited and undisclosed building funds can be used by the national parties to pay for their headquarters, including land, buildings, and equipment. Another notable example of the use of soft money is tax-exempt foundations established by presidential aspirants to fund the preparation for a White House bid. These foundations can also collect unlimited undisclosed amounts from any source. Even though these contributions cannot directly finance presidential campaigns, there is little doubt that they are very beneficial in preparing candidates for the election.

# Assessing the Federal Election Campaign Act

The Federal Election Campaign Act has it supporters and detractors, as does the Federal Election Commission that it established, and even though there has been talk of campaign finance reform for years, there have not been any significant changes since the 1979 amendments.

Most observers agree that the FEC has three principal functions, and of these, it performs quite well in two. The agency receives high marks for its role in administering the public financing of presidential elections. Also, it usually receives praise for its handling of the disclosure of finance information to the press and public. Although there is some debate about just how effective disclosure is in assisting in the enforcement of campaign finance law, as well as acknowledgment that there is sometimes just too much information to analyze thoroughly, it is still fair to say that elections have become more open because citizens and the press now have access to more information about who finances campaigns and how the money is spent.

The major criticism of the FEC involves its third primary role: monitoring and enforcing compliance with the campaign finance law. Critics charge that the agency often fails to act in a timely manner, thereby allowing campaigns to proceed with questionable practices and delaying penalties until long after the election. The

FEC has also been accused of nit-picking on significant details while larger issues, such as the growing underground political economy, go unaddressed. Finally, critics charge that the agency sometimes fails to act evenhandedly when dealing with alleged offenders.

The FEC responds to these criticisms by acknowledging that it has defects and by attempting to correct them. Agency officials also cite their meager budget (approximately $15 million in 1990) and restrictions from FECA and the *Buckley* decision (particularly those limiting contributions but placing few ceilings on expenditures) as factors that limit the agency's monitoring and enforcement capacities.

One change in the campaign-finance law that many experts have suggested is to increase the individual contribution limit from $1,000 to a higher figure to make it more nearly equal to the amount PACs may now contribute and also to take into account the effects of inflation (had it kept pace, this amount would now be at least $2,300). Others advocate requiring more independent expenditures.

Despite the interest in reform, however, difficulties, including partisan divisions in Congress and the constraints of *Buckley,* have led to a continued stalemate on the issue. Consequently, most observers believe that nothing short of a major public scandal would lead to significant reform.

With all FECA's complexities, it is still fair to say that elections have been more open since its passage. Although there are criticisms of some aspects of the campaign finance laws, particularly those dealing with the growth of the underground political economy, observers point out that those very suspicions are valuable in keeping a check on the finance system. Also, it can be said that money does not always ensure political success. Overall, then, the campaign finance system established by FECA and its amendments during the 1970s continued to evolve during the presidential campaigns of the 1980s as candidates and other political activists sought new ways to cope with the various restrictions while at the same time testing their outer limits. As election costs escalated, campaign finance laws did not change. However, the patterns of raising and spending campaign funds by presidential candidates, political parties, PACs, and others changed significantly.

## Notes

1. Herbert Alexander, *Financing the 1984 Election*, p. 81.
2. Alexander Heard, *Made in America: Improving the Nomination and Election of Presidents*, p. 193.
3. Alexander, *Financing the 1984 Election*, p. 42.
4. The Revenue Act of 1971 also allowed taxpayers to claim a tax credit or deduction for contributions to candidates for local, state, or federal office. The deduction portion of this was dropped in 1978, however, and the credit was eliminated in 1986.
5. A multicandidate committee must be registered with the FEC for six months, receive contributions from more than 50 persons, and make contributions to five or more federal candidates.
6. An excellent history and analysis of PACs can be found in the Congressional Research Service publication by Joseph E. Cantor, *Political Action Committees: Their Evolution and Growth and Their Implications for the Political System.*
7. "Persons" can mean individuals or groups. All political committees can also contribute to party committees and to other political committees. Receipts and contributions must be disclosed to the FEC.
8. Alexander, *Financing the 1980 Election*, p. 127, and Harold W. Stanley and Richard G. Niemi, *Vital Statistics on American Politics*, p. 163. (Stanley and Niemi credited this information to Federal Election Commission, "FEC Finds Slower Growth of PAC Activity during 1988 Election," Press Release, April 19, 1989, pp. 1, 7.)

9. Heard, *Made in America,* p. 101. (Heard credited this information to "Court Strikes Down Limits on Independent PAC Outlays," *Congressional Quarterly* 43 (March 23, 1985):532–34; also Alexander, *Financing the 1980 Election,* p. 111; Alexander and Haggerty, *Financing the 1984 Election,* p. 85; and Federal Election Commission release, May 19, 1989.)
10. Rhodes Cook, "The Nominating Process, in *The Elections of 1988,* Michael Nelson, ed., p. 32.
11. Alexander, *Financing the 1984 Election,* p. 54.
12. *Ibid.,* p. 411.
13. Christine Lawrence, ed., *Congressional Quarterly Almanac,* vol. 44 pp. 42–43.

# 6

---

# DELEGATE SELECTION

---

It is far easier and more exciting to follow candidates on the campaign trail than it is to keep up with the ever-changing rules for the selection of delegates to the national party conventions that nominate presidential candidates. But these rules are crucial factors in candidates' development of campaign strategy. This has been especially true since the 1960s because campaign laws and changing party rules have kept the selection process in a state of flux.

In an effort to balance demands for an open nominating process with pressures to keep party alliances in place for the upcoming election, the parties, particularly the Democratic party, have developed nominating processes so complicated that even the professionals need a scorecard to keep track of the game.

## Methods of Choosing Delegates

State law and party rules combine to govern methods of choosing delegates and to determine whether the caucus/convention method, the primary, or a combination of the two is used as a means of picking each state's delegates. The national conventions of both major parties are to be held in the summer of 1992.

Each party bases apportionment of delegates on some combination of population and the relative strength of the party in each state. State parties are allowed to choose among alternatives recommended by the national party committees. In addition, the Democratic party seats appointed delegates and state and local elected officials. Delegations represent specific affirmative action goals for both ethnic minorities and women, but do not have mandatory quotas.[1]

The Republican party specifically awards additional delegates on the basis of a state's having supported Republican candidates for president, senator, governor, and U.S. representative between 1988 and 1991 inclusive.[2]

## PRIMARIES

In a primary, party voters express their preferences for presidential candidates by voting in an election rather than by attending a meeting or a caucus. Primaries were devised during the reformist era of the early twentieth century as one way to take power away from party machines and give the electorate a role in the nominating process. By 1916, 26 states had primary laws on the books, though only some of them applied to the presidential nomination. By 1935, eight states had repealed their primary laws, but after World War II, interest in primaries revived. Election commentaries often cite the high number of primaries in 1976 and 1980—31 and 36, respectively—as a sign of a growing trend. However, these totals included both binding primaries and advisory or nonbinding "beauty contest" primaries.

In 1992, the District of Columbia, Puerto Rico, and 34 states plan to hold primaries (some advisory, some binding). Of these, Democrats prefer the primary in nine states in which Republicans have chosen a caucus or state convention. Thus, the delegate selection process for 1992 promises to remain a mixture of methods.

States not holding primaries to select delegates plan to use caucuses or conventions or a combination of primary and caucus. The delegate selection chart below gives details by state. Republicans will select 2,209 convention delegates and Democrats will seat 4,287 voting delegates, plus alternates.

# Delegate Selection, 1992, By State

The table below lists dates and method of choosing delegates to national nominating conventions and, in some cases, dates of advisory primaries. In the caucus states, where the process extends over a period of days or weeks, the beginning date is generally listed. Dates listed were correct at press time. For questions about particular states, contact the Democratic National Committee, the Republican National Committee, or the state party committees.

| STATE | | NUMBER OF DELEGATE VOTES | DELEGATE SELECTION METHOD | DATE |
|---|---|---|---|---|
| Alabama | D | 62 | Primary | June 2 |
| | R | 38 | Primary | June 2 |
| Alaska | D | 18 | Caucus | April 2 |
| | R | 19 | Caucus | April 23 |
| Arizona | D | 47 | Caucus | March 7 |
| | R | 37 | Caucus | May 1992 |
| Arkansas | D | 43 | Primary | May 26 |
| | R | 27 | District Committees | May 26 |
| California | D | 383 | Primary | June 2 |
| | R | 201 | Primary | June 2 |
| Colorado | D | 54 | Primary | March 3 |
| | R | 37 | Caucus | March 3 |
| Connecticut | D | 61 | Primary | March 24 |
| | R | 35 | Primary | March 24 |
| Delaware | D | 19 | Caucus | March 10 |
| | R | 19 | Caucus | May 1992 |

| STATE | | NUMBER OF DELEGATE VOTES | DELEGATE SELECTION METHOD | DATE |
|-------|---|---|---|---|
| Florida | D | 160 | Primary | March 10 |
| | R | 97 | Primary | March 10 |
| Georgia | D | 88 | Primary | March 10 |
| | R | 52 | Primary | March 10 |
| Hawaii | D | 26 | Caucus | March 10 |
| | R | 14 | Caucus | June 1992 |
| Idaho | D | 24 | Caucus | March 3 |
| | R | 22 | Primary | May 26 |
| Illinois | D | 183 | Primary | March 17 |
| | R | 85 | Primary | March 17 |
| Indiana | D | 87 | Primary | May 5 |
| | R | 51 | Primary | May 5 |
| Iowa | D | 57 | Caucus | February 10 |
| | R | 23 | Caucus | June 12, 13 |
| Kansas | D | 42 | Caucus | March 21 |
| | R | 30 | Caucus | April 7 |
| Kentucky | D | 61 | Primary | May 26 |
| | R | 35 | Caucus | May 26 |
| Louisiana | D | 68 | Primary | March 10 |
| | R | 38 | Caucus | March 10 |
| Maine | D | 30 | Caucus | Feb 23 |
| | R | 22 | Caucus | May 1992 |
| Maryland | D | 79 | Primary | March 3 |
| | R | 42 | Primary | March 3 |
| Massachusetts | D | 106 | Primary | March 10 |
| | R | 38 | Primary | March 10 |
| Michigan | D | 148 | Primary | March 17 |
| | R | 72 | Caucus | March 17 |
| Minnesota | D | 87 | Caucus | March 3 |
| | R | 32 | Caucus | April 7 |
| Mississippi | D | 45 | Primary | March 10 |
| | R | 33 | Primary | March 10 |
| Missouri | D | 86 | Caucus | March 10 |
| | R | 47 | Caucus | May 16–June 27 |
| Montana | D | 22 | Primary | June 2 |
| | R | 20 | Primary | June 2 |
| Nebraska | D | 31 | Primary | May 12 |
| | R | 24 | Primary | May 12 |

| STATE | | NUMBER OF DELEGATE VOTES | DELEGATE SELECTION METHOD | DATE |
|---|---|---|---|---|
| Nevada | D | 24 | Primary | March 8 |
| | R | 21 | Primary | May 7 |
| New Hampshire | D | 24 | Primary | February 18 |
| | R | 23 | Primary | February 18 |
| New Jersey | D | 117 | Primary | June 2 |
| | R | 60 | Primary | June 2 |
| New Mexico | D | 33 | Primary | June 2 |
| | R | 25 | Primary | June 2 |
| New York | D | 268 | Primary | April 7 |
| | R | 100 | Primary | April 7 |
| North Carolina | D | 93 | Primary | May 5 |
| | R | 57 | Primary | May 5 |
| North Dakota | D | 20 | Caucus | March 5–19 |
| | R | 17 | Caucus | April 2 |
| Ohio | D | 167 | Primary | May 5 |
| | R | 83 | Primary | May 5 |
| Oklahoma | D | 53 | Primary | March 10 |
| | R | 34 | Caucus | March 10 |
| Oregon | D | 53 | Primary | May 19 |
| | R | 23 | Primary | May 19 |
| Pennsylvania | D | 188 | Primary | April 28 |
| | R | 91 | Primary | April 28 |
| Rhode Island | D | 28 | Primary | March 10 |
| | R | 15 | Primary | March 10 |
| South Carolina | D | 49 | Primary | March 7 |
| | R | 36 | Caucus | May 2 |
| South Dakota | D | 20 | Primary | February 25 |
| | R | 19 | Primary | February 25 |
| Tennessee | D | 77 | Primary | March 10 |
| | R | 45 | Primary | March 10 |
| Texas | D | 214 | Caucus/ Primary | March 10 |
| | R | 121 | Caucus | March 10 |
| Utah | D | 28 | Caucus | March 3 |
| | R | 27 | Caucus | June 1992 |
| Vermont | D | 20 | Caucus | March 31 |
| | R | 19 | Caucus | May 16 |

| STATE | | NUMBER OF DELEGATE VOTES | DELEGATE SELECTION METHOD | DATE |
|---|---|---|---|---|
| Virginia | **D** | 92 | Caucus | April 11 |
| | **R** | 55 | Caucus | June 6 |
| Washington | **D** | 80 | Caucus | March 3 |
| | **R** | 35 | Caucus | May 19 |
| West Virginia | **D** | 39 | Primary | May 12 |
| | **R** | 18 | Primary | May 12 |
| Wisconsin | **D** | 91 | Primary | April 7 |
| | **R** | 35 | Primary/ Caucus | April 7/April–May |
| Wyoming | **D** | 19 | Caucus | March 7 |
| | **R** | 20 | Caucus | May 1 & 2 |
| District of Columbia | **D** | 30 | Primary | May 5 |
| | **R** | 14 | Primary | May 5 |
| American Samoa | **D** | 4 | Caucus | May 3 |
| Democrats Abroad | **D** | 9 | Caucus | March 7–9 |
| Guam | **D** | 4 | Caucus | May 3 |
| | **R** | 4 | Caucus | TBD |
| Puerto Rico | **D** | 57 | Primary | March 15 |
| | **R** | 14 | Primary | March 15 |
| Virgin Islands | **D** | 4 | Caucus | March 28 |
| | **R** | 4 | Caucus | TBD |

Key: D = Democrat R = Republican
*Sources:* Republican National Committee and Democratic National Committee.

## PRIMARY TERMINOLOGY

To understand news reports and political commentators when they talk about primaries, it helps to have a quick definition of key terms:

- *Open primary:* Permits voting in that primary by any registered voter regardless of party. Such primaries are not favored by party leaders. The Democratic National Committee has ruled that primaries held in open primary states are not binding on the selection of delegates.

- *Closed primary:* Restricts voting in that primary to voters who have registered in advance as being affiliated with that party.
- *Direct presidential preference primary:* Lists all party candidates for presidential nomination on the party ballot. Some preferential primaries are binding, some are advisory. Delegates are selected at a caucus after the primary.
- *Winner-take-all:* All delegates go to the primary winner. In 1992, only the Republican primary in California will be of this type. The Democrats do not permit winner-take-all primaries.
- *Direct delegate selection:* Voters vote for the delegates themselves as listed on the ballot. Generally, the name of the presidential candidate supported by a particular delegate is also listed on the ballot. This makes it easier for voters to coordinate their own presidential preferences with their votes for delegates. Democratic party candidates have the right of prior approval of all delegates listed as supporting them on the primary ballots.
- *Proportional:* After the voters vote for presidential candidates, the delegates are allotted on the basis of the proportions of the vote won by the various candidates. Distribution may be statewide or by district (congressional or other) within a state. It also may be partly district, partly statewide.

A number of states have taken steps to move up their preliminary selection dates for the 1992 campaign. Nine states have moved their primary/caucus dates from April–June to February and March. Of these, South Dakota's jump from June to February 25 is the most dramatic. Western states have tended to consolidate toward March 3, including changed dates in Colorado, Idaho, Utah,

and Washington. The traditional southern "Super Tuesday" primary date, scheduled for March 10, has also picked up more states:
Louisiana, Tennessee, and Texas, all changing from May selection
dates.

## CAUCUS/CONVENTION

In the caucus/convention method of choosing delegates to
national party conventions, the following persons can meet together at the precinct level:

- Those registered in that party,
- Anyone who voted in the last primary, and
- In some states, anyone who is willing to sign a pledge that
  he or she is a bona fide party member.

Party rules require caucus dates, times, and places to be pub-
licized in advance. Delegates to county conventions then select
representatives to go on to district and state conventions.

Usually, prospective delegates' presidential preferences are
known or declared; delegates may also run as undecided. In any
case, those attending the meetings have a clear knowledge of who,
if anyone, these delegates will back when they reach the national
nominating convention.

Under party rules, Democrats must choose their delegates
according to proportional representation at each level; that is, delegates selected to go on to the next level must fairly reflect the
proportion of support that each presidential candidate or the undecided block has won at the meeting.

Since 1984, the Democrats have allowed for a new option at
the statewide level. In some cases, when three or more delegates
are to be chosen, one delegate can be allocated to the front-runner,
with the remaining delegates apportioned among the leading contenders. A few states have opted for such a process; all others use

the direct or proportional method. The Democratic rules stipulate that in each state, a candidate must receive a minimum percentage of support in order to be represented.

# Party Reform

The delegate selection processes of the political parties were not immune to the political ferment associated with the Vietnam War and civil rights protests of the 1960s. Focusing public attention on governmental and political process, critics directed attention to the fact that the method of selecting delegates to the nominating conventions of both major parties tended to underrepresent women, minorities, and young people. Subsequently, both parties undertook reform measures to make delegate selection processes more accessible.

## DEMOCRATS

The contentious 1968 Democratic National Convention in Chicago, and Hubert Humphrey's defeat by Richard Nixon in the subsequent election, generated demands for reform that were reflected in the 1972 Democratic National Convention delegate selection process. The two most controversial changes were:

- The encouragement of more participation by, and representation of, young people, women, and racial minorities by requiring state delegations to represent the proportions of these categories in that state's population; and
- The limiting of the number of delegates selected by state party committees to 10 percent of the total delegation.

In 1976, the Democratic National Committee revised the rules governing the selection of delegates to require affirmative action plans. The portion of delegates that state party committees could select was increased from 10 percent to 25 percent. Significant rule changes continued in 1980 when state delegations had to be equally divided between men and women and the time period during which delegates could be chosen was shortened to three months between the second Tuesday in March and the second Tuesday in June. Only registered Democrats could vote in Democratic primaries, and state delegations had to reflect the proportion of the vote that each candidate received in the primary election or state caucus. To respond to criticisms that earlier reforms had worked to exclude party and elected officials from the process, the number of delegates was increased by 10 percent to allow more elected party and state officials to be included.

In 1984, after Jimmy Carter's second-term loss in 1980, the Democratic party set up a Commission on Presidential Nomination, headed by North Carolina Governor James B. Hunt, to take another look at the whole delegate selection question. The Commission was unable to fully achieve one of its stated goals—a shortened campaign season. But it did make substantial changes in the rules designed to lessen the likelihood of a dark-horse candidate capitalizing on the momentum gained by early victories in the Iowa caucuses and the New Hampshire primary.

In 1992, as a result of the Hunt Commission changes, 12 weeks are set aside as the "window" during which all delegate selection must occur. Only days separate the Iowa caucuses from the primary in New Hampshire in 1992. By the end of March, 66 percent of voting delegates will have been selected, compared to 42 percent at the same point in the 1980 campaign.

## REPUBLICANS

Republicans also responded to the reform sentiment that was prevalent in the late 1960s, although their reforms were more cautious than those of the Democrats. Basically, the Republican rules adopted by the 1976 Convention govern the delegate selection process.

Republicans call on state party organizations to take "positive action" to achieve broad participation by women, young people, minorities, "heritage groups," and senior citizens. The Republican National Committee urges equal representation of men and women. No mechanism exists to mandate compliance with these standards. Other reforms include bans on proxy voting and on ex-officio or automatic "senior party official" delegates. Republicans have made efforts to make party meetings more public and visible.

The Republican party operates under a somewhat different set of premises than the Democratic party. Republicans believe that national party leadership must not dictate to state party processes. The result is that the Republican National Committee recommends, but does not require, that reforms and changes be made by the state and local party units to ensure broad-based participation in party processes.

# Evaluating the Selection Process

Both the primary system and the caucus/convention system of choosing delegates to the national conventions have their strong and weak points. Some people wonder whether the primaries have actually achieved the initial goal of democratizing participation in the delegate selection process, since voter turnout in primary elections is low compared to turnout in general elections. Only about 25 percent of the voting-age population votes in primaries.

It is true that primary elections appeal to highly motivated voters. Scholars have found that the average primary voter tends to be slightly better educated, more affluent, and older than the average voter in general elections. Primary voters also are more likely to be interested in a particular candidate or to have strong party ties.

Observers also note that a grueling series of primary elections, extending from the winter of a presidential election year to the summer, places a tremendous drain on candidates and campaign personnel, to say nothing of campaign funds. Reformers have long suggested shortening the primary election campaign period to take account of all these problems. The trend toward early primary dates in February and March, combined with regional selection dates, such as "Super Tuesday" in the South, may be beneficial in that direction.

Supporters of primary elections cite the fact that they offer relatively unknown candidates a chance to build their credibility and to assess their general popularity and intraparty strength, and perhaps to capture the nomination through a series of early primary victories. But others point out that the primary process diminishes the influence in the nominating process of state and local party officials as well as members of Congress, persons who generally have a realistic view of presidential leadership skills.

Critics of the caucus/convention method of selecting delegates to national conventions stress that participation in caucuses/conventions involves an even lower percentage of persons than is the case in primary elections. However, caucuses at the community level can help build party unity.

All in all, no one advocates returning to the practices of a past era, when smoke-filled rooms and secret deals for deciding presidential nominations were the common *modus operandi*.

## Notes

1. Democratic Party of the U.S., *Delegate Selection Rules for the 1992 Democratic National Convention*, pp. 4–7.
2. Republican National Committee, *How a President Is Nominated and Selected*.

# 7

---

# THE CONVENTION

---

"Several thousand people, most of them parochial in outlook and strangers to one another... thrown together for a few days to make a set of major decisions, under conditions of great strain and maximum publicity."[1] That is how Judith N. Parris, one of the best writers on the subject, describes the quadrennial rite of the national political party conventions.

Well in advance of the meeting date, each national committee selects a city for the convention site. Local pride and the prospect of increased business induce many cities to lobby for the honor. The national committees make their selections on the basis of convenience, available accommodations, and political considerations. The sheer size of the conventions limits the sites to those cities with major convention facilities. In 1992, the Democrats will meet July 13–16 in New York City, and the Republicans will meet August 17–20 in Houston, Texas.

---

# Functions of National Conventions

National conventions have no formal standing in the election process defined in the Constitution. Without the work done by the conventions, however, there would be no true national parties. Conventions make their own rules and are the supreme authority over other components of the national parties, including the national committees. They are exercises in power both on and off the convention floor.

As indicated in Chapter 6, Democrats maintain strict control over the rules by which delegates are chosen, as well as over committee structure and other internal affairs; Republicans usually leave this type of decision to their state committees. Regardless of the methods used, parties have few ways to enforce their decisions other than to refuse credentials or admittance at future conventions to a violator. In many cases, the lengthy preparations that precede conventions enable differences within the party to be sorted out before they surface on the convention floor.

The convention performs four major functions.

1. *It nominates candidates for president and vice president.* Major party nominees can depend on having their names— and/or a slate of electors pledged to them—on the November election ballot in all states, a luxury not easy for a minor party or independent candidate to come by. Formal nomination by a major party is a practical necessity for candidates because of the existence of a massive, nationwide electorate. Candidates could be nominated in other ways, such as by a state-by-state direct primary, but that method would rob the major national parties of much of their role and influence. Formal major party nomination also qualifies the Republican and Democratic nominees for public funding of their general election campaigns, unless they opt for a privately funded campaign.
2. *It adopts a national party platform.* Although the platform

is not binding on members of the party, it does establish a tone and a direction behind which most party members can rally, and it serves a number of other purposes that will be discussed later. After the election, presidents, senators, and representatives interpret the platform to suit their own needs and philosophies.

**3.** *It governs the party.* Policies and procedures for the next convention are adopted and study groups may be appointed. For Democrats, all state nominations for national committee members must be approved by the national convention, thus providing leadership for the next four years. Republicans rely on state law and/or state party rules in this regard.

**4.** *It rallies the party faithful.* It can provide a time for the healing of wounds that may have been opened during the nomination campaign and can bring factions together behind a ticket. Up to the time of the convention, contenders have vied for delegate votes; after the convention they must present a united front to win the votes of citizens.

# The Gathering of the Delegates

A convention city on the eve of a meeting is a center of activity and expectancy. Delegations are as different from one another as the states they represent. Some hold meetings to choose their leaders—chair, vice chair, and secretary—before they leave home. Others wait until they arrive to take care of these matters. Until modern reforms, delegates were usually upper-middle class, college-educated professionals or managers; many were professional politicians or elected officials, and most of them were male. Frequently, delegates have had limited previous acquaintance with other members of their own delegation.

Soon after arrival, preliminary conferences and caucuses begin.

Each state delegation has its own headquarters to direct activities such as meeting with candidates and issuing press releases. Meeting at the same time, and competing with state caucuses for the presence of delegates, are representatives of labor, business, agriculture, religious, or other interests. Many of these groups hope to influence both the choice of candidates and the planks that make up the party platform. Spokespersons for these groups may have already testified at hearings of the platform committees, held months before.

Electronic broadcast equipment is already in place at the convention hall and in main meeting rooms and hotels. Because of the huge radio and television audience that will be tuned in throughout the convention, each step of the meeting is planned down to the minute. However, prolonged credentials arguments, spontaneous demonstrations, or other unforeseen circumstances often disrupt the most careful of plans.

In 1972, even though strategists had planned for George McGovern to deliver his acceptance speech in prime time (around 10:00 p.m. EST), a floor dispute preceding the speech lasted into the early morning hours. By the time McGovern finally made his speech, most of the television audience had gone to bed.

In recent years, much of the convention work is a *fait accompli* weeks before the convention date. State laws and convention rules to commit delegates' votes determine the nominations of presidential candidates long before the delegates meet. In fact, in 1988 both potential nominees for the major parties announced their vice presidential choices prior to the conventions.

## Convention Makeup

Long before convention time each party will have decided how many people—voting delegates or otherwise—will be admitted to the convention and how the total number will be apportioned among the states. This allocation is announced in the "Final Call to Convention" and is sent to state and local parties long before the selection process begins.

Critics often have complained that the thousands of people in attendance at conventions make meaningful deliberation impossible. They have recommended smaller conventions with fewer delegate votes and fewer alternates. Most party leaders have argued, however, that there must be enough delegate votes to be representative of the national constituency that makes up the party. Additionally, a smaller convention would reduce the number of faithful workers who look forward to a place in a delegation as a reward for dedicated service. Being chosen as a delegate is often a mixed reward; delegates must pay their own way to and from the convention as well as for accommodations while there.

In 1992, close to 5,000 delegates and alternates will attend the Democratic convention in New York City. This is a continuing downward trend in attendance from 5,400 in 1980 and 5,200 in 1984. Republicans will send 2,209 representatives and a like number of alternates to Houston.

In apportioning delegate votes to the states, the national parties have generally been guided by two considerations: the population of the state and the voting strength of the party in that state. Population has been recognized by factoring in the state electoral vote; party strength has been recognized by giving bonus delegates to states where the party did well in recent elections.

The Ripon Society, an organization of Republican liberals, challenged its party's 1976 bonus system by arguing that it discriminates against larger states by reducing their influence. Specifically, California, with nearly 10 percent of the nation's population, got only 7.5 percent of the 1976 Republican convention delegates. New York, with 9 percent of the population, got only 6.8 percent of the delegate vote. The U.S. Court of Appeals for the District of Columbia upheld the old formula, saying that, under the First Amendment, political parties can manage their own affairs without interference from the courts.

Sometimes the choice of a nominee has been effectively determined before the convention, as in the case of an incumbent president. In that case, the delegates play a ratifying role. If no clear front-runner has emerged by the end of June, the delegates have a time of decision ahead of them during which preconvention caucuses and special-interest gatherings take on new importance.

Before 1952, "brokered" conventions were common. Behind-the-scenes deals were often made, votes were traded, and a compromise candidate frequently was chosen from the pack as the nominee. Since then, neither party has taken more than one ballot to choose a presidential nominee. Indeed, presidential nominees are well-known due to the state primaries and media coverage. Thus the convention delegates confirm, rather than choose, the front-runner.

## Committee Work

Much of the preliminary work of the conventions is done by committees. The Democrats have three standing committees—credentials, platform, and rules—and one special committee—arrangements—to administer the operations of the convention. There are four committees in the Republican party, focusing on credentials, resolutions (platform), rules and order of business, and permanent organization.

### DEMOCRATIC PARTY

The party's standing committees have a total of 159 members; 156 of them are voting members. One hundred thirty-one votes are allocated among states and territories by the same formula used to determine the size of national convention delegations; membership from each state or territory must be equally divided between men and women. Committee members are chosen by delegations to represent their presidential preferences proportionally.

The remaining 25 voting members of each committee are chosen by the Executive Committee of the Democratic National Committee to represent party and elected officials and do not favor any presidential candidate. Members of the standing committees need not be delegates or alternates to the national convention. Meetings are open to the public.

The convention has final authority over decisions and recommendations of standing committees. The standing committees perform the following functions:

- The Credentials Committee recommends to the convention the resolution of any challenges involving delegates chosen for the convention.
- The Platform Committee prepares the party platform, with the views of all presidential candidates taken into consideration. A minority report can reach the convention floor, but only if 25 percent of the committee members agree.
- The Rules Committee recommends the permanent rules of the convention, the agenda, the permanent officers of the convention, and amendments to the charter of the party. It can offer resolutions on matters that do not fall under the purview of the other convention committees.

## REPUBLICAN PARTY

In 1992, the Republicans will retain their practice of having one man and one woman from each state delegation serve on each committee. Each state also gets one additional delegate representative to each committee. The District of Columbia, Puerto Rico, the Virgin Islands, and Guam are each allotted one seat on each of the committees as well. If a state delegation is too small for both a man and a woman to serve on all convention committees, then the delegation may allocate its appointments in any way it chooses.

The Credentials Committee receives and monitors credentials of all delegates and alternates and determines the permanent roll of the convention. If there is a challenge the Republican National Committee makes every effort to resolve it before the convention convenes, although disputes may be brought to the floor.

The Resolutions Committee drafts the party platform for the next four years. Months before the convention begins, research is begun and preliminary work gets under way, with subcommittees focusing on various issues.

The Committee on Rules and Order of Business drafts the rules to be adopted by the convention covering proceedings, organization of the national committee, and attendance at the next convention.

The Permanent Organization Committee recommends a set of officers for the convention, the most important of whom is the permanent chair.

# The Convention Begins

The permanent convention chair has traditionally been chosen ahead of the convention by consultation among party leaders. The convention merely ratifies the choice after it is presented. Since fairness to all factions by the presiding officer is a must if the convention is not to be disrupted, persons of stature and moderation are chosen—present and former Speakers of the House of Representatives are especially favored.

When a convention begins, the national committee chair soon yields the gavel to a temporary chair picked in advance by the national committee. He or she presides while housekeeping matters are taken care of and then yields to the permanent chair, who presides during the platform debates and the nominating activities. The first highlight of the national convention is the "keynote address," usually given by the temporary chair. Many up-and-coming politicians have launched their careers by means of a rousing keynote speech. For example, Governor Mario Cuomo of New York has been a popular potential Democratic candidate ever since his keynote address at the 1984 national convention in San Francisco.

Following the keynote, delegate credentials and convention rules are accepted. At this point, any credentials battles between slates of delegates will be brought before the convention for decision if neither the national committee nor the credentials committee has been able to iron out the dispute.

Next, the platform committee reads its report. The significance of the platform does not lie in the fact that it will bind the nominees to a program. What is important is that the planks indicate which faction will control the nomination, especially if great differences exist among the contenders. In 1980, for example, Republicans removed a plank that had been in the platform for years—support for the Equal Rights Amendment; it was a clear signal that the conservative philosophy would prevail.

A platform may also serve a symbolic purpose by providing an occasion for debate that allows dissidents to vent their grievances. This then is the first step toward an important convention purpose: closing ranks behind the slate in order to win the general election.

# Nominating the President

While debates over housekeeping matters and the platform are going on, delegations will caucus and then caucus again. Presidential hopefuls and those empowered to speak for them will try to build their delegate strength. Promises will be made and, perhaps, bargains struck. The candidates operate by phone or through representatives. Traditionally it has been considered bad form for candidates to appear at the convention hall before nominations are made. With the final platform plank completed, attention will turn to the convention's chief purpose, the nomination of the presidential candidate.

The candidate's name is placed in nomination by a prominent supporter. The order of nominations is determined by lot for the Democrats. Republicans hold a roll call by state.

The nominating speech for each candidate is traditionally followed by a demonstration of support from backers plus a series of seconding speeches. Again, because of the role of television and the desire to have the nominee speak before the largest possible audience, both parties now put time limits on the nominating speeches and the demonstrations.

Both parties also have attempted to keep frivolous candidates from being nominated by requiring candidates to present evidence of substantial support before their names can be placed in nomination.

After the close of nominations, the roll of the states for the casting of votes is called. Lengthy speeches by a delegation chair when announcing the state's vote or the polling of each member of the delegation is discouraged. A state may pass when its turn comes and then vote at the end of the roll call or may switch its vote before the final tally is announced. These measures are sometimes used as tactical maneuvers for a favored candidate or as a way of jumping on the bandwagon of a winning candidate.

In both parties, a majority vote is now sufficient to nominate. If no candidate receives a majority on the first ballot, the roll is called again until someone does receive a majority. Previously, under the Democrats' unit rule, a majority of one in a delegation could swing the entire delegation's voting strength behind a particular candidate, but this is no longer permitted. Republicans never used a unit rule.

While the roll call of states edges along in a close ballot, millions of people all over the country mark convention tally sheets as they watch on television or listen to the radio. When a state delegation's vote finally carries a candidate past the tip point to victory, pandemonium breaks loose in the convention hall, often making it a difficult feat for the chair to finish calling the roll. Although loudly celebrating the party's choice, delegates and viewers in recent years have rarely been surprised at the outcome.

# Choosing the Vice President

One more task faces the delegates before they can head for home: to nominate a candidate for vice president. The official nomination, as in the case of the presidential candidate, is made by state roll call, but the procedure is admittedly less suspenseful. Traditionally, the wishes of the presidential nominee are honored in the choice of a running mate. That choice is known to all by roll call time so that the nomination is only a formality and is sometimes made by acclamation.

Occasionally there is some grumbling from delegates and even a battle for the nomination—in 1956 at the Democratic convention presidential nominee Adlai Stevenson threw the vice presidential nomination open to the convention.

The selection of a vice presidential nominee usually has been largely a matter of balancing the election ticket for maximum vote-getting potential. Accordingly, in 1988, New Englander Michael Dukakis, a fairly liberal Democrat, chose Senator Lloyd Bentsen of Texas, considered more conservative. That same year, George Bush, with ties to both New England and Texas, chose a midwesterner, Senator Dan Quayle, as his running mate. However, this did not broaden his ideological base, since both are considered conservative Republicans.

The Constitution assigns the vice president very few duties other than to succeed to the office of president if it becomes vacant or if the president becomes disabled and is unable to function as president. But the office, which rarely got much attention in the past, has become more important in recent years in the eyes of the electorate. Franklin Roosevelt's death while in office, Eisenhower's serious illnesses, Kennedy's assassination, Nixon's resignation, and the attempt on Reagan's life all indicate that the individual chosen to fill the vice presidential role must be of presidential quality.

Throughout his term of office, President Carter regularly assigned broad responsibilities to Vice President Mondale and kept him informed on a daily basis—in marked contrast to the treatment of previous vice presidents. President Ronald Reagan gave Vice President George Bush a major role as spokesperson for his administration. However, Bush, as president, has not provided as many expanded opportunities of importance for Vice President Dan Quayle.

Leaders in both parties have looked thoughtfully at the vice presidential selection process, questioning the haste sometimes shown in choosing a president's running mate. Many critics have questioned the fact that the victorious presidential nominee does the choosing, leaving delegates no role except to endorse. Criticism does not end there. Others have continued to question the role of the vice president; historian Arthur Schlesinger, Jr., has called for abolition of the office, and others have proposed multiple vice presidents to share the work of administering the executive branch.

## The Acceptance Speech

The final big moment for the convention is the acceptance speech, which sets the tone for the election campaign, by the presidential nominee. This custom is comparatively new. Before 1932, candidates did not go to conventions. Rather, delegations were sent to inform winners of their nominations. In 1932, Franklin D. Roosevelt broke that tradition and flew to Chicago to accept the nomination personally, and all candidates have done so since.

## Mass Media at the National Conventions

Along with party reforms, radio and television have removed much of the secret, smoke-filled room atmosphere from the national conventions. Television, with its live coverage of events in and around the convention hall, has brought the proceedings into millions of homes.

As a result, there are often more media representatives at the convention than there are delegates, a situation that many critics call a case of the tail wagging the dog. They complain that the television networks often cut away from convention proceedings to present their own interviews, profiles, and special reports. The careful viewer is likely to know as much or more than the delegates about the convention strategies and events.

Television networks ABC, NBC, and CBS have announced the end of gavel-to-gavel coverage of the national conventions. However, Americans who have cable TV will most likely see complete coverage of the 1992 conventions on CNN and/or C-SPAN.

# The Future of National Conventions

American political scientists are debating whether national political conventions will be necessary in the twenty-first century. There is speculation that eventually conventions will be replaced by a national presidential primary. David Broder, nationally syndicated columnist, has written, "the parties increasingly have lost their place in a politics dominated by individual candidates, mass-media messages, and the maneuverings of organized interest groups."[2]

## *Notes*

**1.** Judith N. Parris, *The Convention Problem,* p. 4.
**2.** David S. Broder, "Conventions Losing Their Surprises," September 4, 1991, Washington Post Writers Group.

# 8

## THE GENERAL ELECTION CAMPAIGN

$T$raditionally, candidates have spent the time between their nominations and Labor Day—the calm eye of the campaign hurricane—resting, planning strategy for the upcoming two campaign months, and making last-minute staff changes. Which political bases to touch, how to spread financial resources, how best to use the media, how to make use of celebrity endorsements, and how to motivate and organize local or state party workers are all decisions that must be reaffirmed before the final push.

At this point, too, candidates and voters alike have become weary, having gone through many months of increasing political activity. The print and broadcast media have been saturated with political advertising, analysis, and campaign news since before the primary season began. Now, new enthusiasm must be generated for the crucial general election campaign.

Nominees must unite their parties and reorganize and supplement their staffs by recruiting from the ranks of their defeated rivals. They must strive to keep damaging or embarrassing incidents to a minimum while trying to win over the undecided, apathetic, or hostile voters who can decide a close election. All this is prelude to the presidential campaign, a time when the nation seems to pause, reexamine its needs and goals, and, with the alternatives narrowed down, prepare to select a leader.

# Campaign Organization

The principal purpose of a presidential campaign is to win votes by appealing to as many kinds of people as possible in as many different ways as possible. To do this with a potential electorate of more than 185 million people is a staggering task that demands good organization, a large staff, and a great deal of money. The day of the "front-porch campaign" is over. In 1860 Abraham Lincoln won the election for the Republican party without leaving Springfield, Illinois, or making a single speech. One hundred years later, Republican nominee Richard Nixon traveled 65,000 miles, made 212 speeches, visited all 50 states—and lost.

Since Eisenhower entered politics in 1952, presidential candidates have created national organizations, independent of the national and state party organizations, to run their campaigns. The Federal Election Campaign Act (FECA) has made the establishment of such committees mandatory for handling campaign contributions and expenditures. As campaigns have grown more complex, campaign organizations have become more professional, relying on political consultants, media experts, and pollsters to provide information and advice. A close watch is kept on the nation's mood and the opponent's progress, so that strategy and tactics can quickly be altered to meet changing circumstances.

Campaign organizations vary in structure. However, most include a director and manager at the national level who supervise the work of numerous specialists, such as schedulers, public relations experts, issue advisors, and speech writers. Campaign staffs keep in close touch with special-interest groups such as minorities, unions, or small-business owners. A field coordinator maintains contact with state campaign and party committees. The treasurer keeps financial records and sees that Federal Election Commision (FEC) reports are filed.

Campaign organizations work with the media watching their every move. Dissension and confusion in the ranks are quickly reported, with the implication drawn that a candidate who cannot run a campaign organization will not be able to run the country. Reporters also watch the campaign funding process.

As party regulars have had less to say in the selection of the party's standard-bearer, candidates have become increasingly independent. Reagan in 1980 and Carter in 1976 ran as party "outsiders" and tended to rely on their own primary campaign staffs from California and Georgia, respectively. The parties, however, do provide volunteer help, contacts, get-out-the-vote and registration drives, campaign paraphernalia such as buttons and bumper stickers, opinion research, publicity, and other resources, including contributions of funds as permitted under FECA. The successful campaign committee will also find a way to tap volunteer resources while ensuring that the presidential nominee and the nominee's campaign manager retain overall control.

The state and local party organizations, from central committee to precinct level, play an important role in the campaign. They keep up enthusiasm at the grass roots, distribute campaign literature, and provide staff for headquarters and polling places. Good advance work and cooperation with state and local party volunteers and elected officials are important to make a campaign tour effective. The organization at the local level also keeps national headquarters informed about which bases must be touched and which fences need mending.

There are two kinds of volunteer groups in a presidential campaign. First are the party-affiliated groups such as Young Democrats or Young Republicans, State Federation of Republican or Democratic Women, and local or district Democratic or Republican clubs. These groups are organizationally separate from the parties but work closely with them. A second type is the "Citizens for John Doe Club." Such groups spring to life in every presidential campaign and are kept organizationally distinct for several reasons. They provide a way for volunteers to work for the national ticket without working for all party candidates, and they also may provide a special way to appeal to specific groups such as ethnic minorities or professional organizations. In 1960, for example, some 200 local-level Viva Kennedy clubs were organized in the 21 states with high concentrations of Spanish-speaking citizens.

Both parties also receive help in the form of money and volunteers from the major interest groups such as labor, business, and agriculture. (See Chapter 5 regarding the activities of corporate and union political action committees and the role that independent expenditures can play.) No party can depend upon undivided support from any interest group, however; labor unions, for example, have long been a prime source of support for the Democratic party, but their efforts were divided in 1980 and 1984 when many rank-and-file union members overrode their national leadership to work and vote for Ronald Reagan. The business community, often thought of as being pro-Republican, also makes contributions to the Democrats.

# Campaign Strategy

Campaign strategy is an overall plan to use the available resources and the strengths of the candidate to the best advantage to win the requisite number of electoral votes to be elected president of the United States. It is developed from lessons learned in the successful campaign for the nomination and the expertise of the pollsters, analysts, and consultants working with the campaign organization.

Campaign strategy is influenced by many factors—whether or not an incumbent is in the race, the candidate's personal qualities, the role of the media, the interpretation of the latest poll results, the mood of the country, the economic climate, and even events overseas. It must be constantly revised and refocused to keep pace with changing conditions. For example, the presidential campaign in 1980 was greatly affected by the Iranian hostage crisis that was taking place at the same time. The general peace and prosperity in 1984 and 1988 affected those campaigns, and in 1992 the state of the economy and foreign policy are sure once again to be important issues.

New campaign finance rules have a profound effect on strategy. One of the first major decisions a campaign organization must make is whether to accept federal funds and the accompanying limitations on campaign contributions and expenditures or to operate with private financing. Recently, candidates have chosen to take advantage of the federal funding option and leave supplementary fund-raising to the regular party organization and independent committees.

The work begun during the convention—uniting the party behind a single candidate after what may have been a bitter fight for the nomination—must continue. This effort and the drive to mobilize supporters and capture the electoral votes of key states determine campaign travel plans and scheduling. Candidates concentrate efforts on swing states, make only token appearances in states where they are assured of victory, and concede those states where they have little chance to win. This planning is done against a background of party officials clamoring for an appearance by the standard-bearer in their states to motivate party workers, increase interest and turnout, and boost the campaigns of the party's contenders for state and local offices. It is also planned within the framework of limited financial resources, time, and the candidate's stamina.

Candidates must determine the image they wish to project and how best to bring their message to as many potential voters as possible, knowing that voters base their decisions on the candidate's party, stand on issues, and leadership qualities. They must decide how to appeal to all factions within their own parties while also attracting independents and dissatisfied voters from other parties. Democratic candidates start with a larger party base (see Chapter 3) and can make a more partisan appeal; Republicans must appeal to a broader range of the electorate. Incumbent contenders often choose to appear "presidential" and seek to be portrayed as too busy with important official duties to take to the campaign trail.

On issues, candidates can either appeal to a broad coalition of voters by blurring their stands on controversial issues or try to appeal to special interests by taking a bold and forthright stand. Often this decision has already been made by the selection of a nominee from either the broad mainstream of the party or the more extreme margins.

During the nominating process it is crucial for candidates to mobilize early support from a squadron of devoted workers and the voters who turn out for primaries and caucuses. Thus, candidates are motivated to take strong stands in order to appeal to a dedicated group of zealous supporters in the initial stages of their campaigns. But they must also allow for flexibility later on, when they need to appeal to a broader electorate, without appearing to renege on earlier commitments.

Political writer Richard Reeves suggests that the most successful politician may be the candidate who creates no enemies—the lowest common denominator.[1] And Alex Armedaris, president of a campaign management firm, advises candidates to sound as if they are saying something but actually to say nothing: "A strong position on an issue will only turn voters off." For instance, during the 1984 campaign Walter Mondale took specific stands on several controversial issues, including a proposal to raise taxes. His loss in that election showed other candidates the wisdom of remaining cautious about taking unpopular stands on policy issues.

Projecting a presidential "image" has become increasingly important as more voters receive their information and impressions from television. Candidates seek to appear decisive, competent, and assertive, and television ads have been turned to as the best way for the campaign organization to present its candidate as it wants him or her to be perceived. An important strategic decision is how much television and other advertising will be used, as well as when and where to target it. Because media advertising is so expensive, it must be distributed carefully throughout the campaign period so momentum is built early and sustained and then followed by a media blitz just before the election.

Finally, two other campaign strategies have gained popularity in recent years: running a negative campaign and focusing on symbolic issues. In the first case, a candidate attacks his opponent's competence and character, which under some circumstances may be legitimate, but more often is misleading and plays on the voters' emotions. In the latter, a candidate emphasizes an issue such as patriotism, which has strong emotional appeal for most voters, but neglects more serious issues, such as the federal budget deficit. Critics charge that this pervasive use of negative and symbolic themes shortchanges the voters.

## Campaign Tactics

While campaign strategy looks at the big picture, campaign tactics govern the day-to-day activities that implement the strategy. Even more than strategy, tactics must be flexible and able to be changed quickly as events warrant. Whereas strategy is developed and controlled from the national campaign headquarters, tactical considerations often determine the actions of the national and state party organizations, state and local campaign offices, and volunteer and independent committees.

Successful tactics include careful advance work that guarantees a full house at a campaign appearance or frequent "media opportunities" that show the candidate acting "presidential" or interacting with citizens who belong to important minority or ethnic groups. Methods of bringing the candidate's message and image before the voters range from leaflets passed out or distributed door-to-door by volunteers to nationwide television ads. Celebrity endorsements and special appearances have become important features of campaigns.

Even if the candidate's campaign committee is not soliciting contributions, the party and independent committees are doing so, using traditional techniques such as fundraisers and new tactics such as sophisticated, computerized direct-mail appeals. At the same time, such committees are deciding how best to help their candidate through advertising, financing opinion polls, setting up telephone banks to identify supporters, or recruiting volunteers.

Tactical decisions also may govern how time, money, paid and volunteer staff, and the candidate's energy will be allocated. This involves targeting—expanding effort where it will be most effective rather than trying to cover all areas and groups. Opinion polling can reveal those who are already in the candidate's corner and those who could not be won over by any action, thus helping campaigns target their resources. They can also show where extra advertising would be useful.

Because the last few national elections have shown that women are now voting in greater proportions and that they tend to vote on the basis of issue stands that often differ from those of men (creating the so-called gender gap), targeting will no doubt be directed toward women in the 1992 presidential campaign. Political advisors and leaders of women's groups point out that the majority of voters now are women, a factor that candidates cannot ignore. Other groups such as blacks, Hispanics, and older citizens are beginning to capitalize on the importance of voting to achieve their ends.

As the campaign draws to a close, the last step is to translate support into votes. Last-minute television appeals, phone calls from volunteers, and door-to-door canvassing are used to urge registered voters to go to the polls. Campaign workers offer rides and child care and hand out leaflets outside the polling places. In the final analysis, the success of a campaign effort is measured very simply: by victory or defeat.

## In Campaigning

rn about candidates through direct
ts left at their doors, most informa-
s comes through the mass media—
and magazines. The way the media
vay the candidates use paid media
fference in election results.

### COVERAGE

ia, covering a presidential campaign
of conducting a major military cam-
ent a significant organizational chal-
begin as long as two years before the
zations have the ability to determine
a campaign—the ability to mold
y up some candidates and play down
he results of primaries, to generate a
or impending defeat.

r, journalists must make some key
ge should each candidate receive?
t the candidates say in official posi-
s cover details of what candidates
aigning or their records in office?
ake analytical interpretations of can-
s?

gn reporting ebbs and flows, depen-
dates, the events of a campaign, and
, Theodore White put his imprint on
nicle of the Kennedy/ Nixon race in
In a reporting classic, he laid out a
ical campaigning was all about—
d around a hectic scramble for the

Since then, in-depth reporting has examined candidates' personalities and life-styles, scrutinized family life, and watched campaign organizations for signs of trouble or changes in direction. Greater emphasis has also been placed on the "horse race" aspects of the campaigns. Reporters tend to focus their attention on the candidates' strategies and errors as well as on who is leading in the latest polls. However, some within the media industry feel that attention to such matters obscures serious coverage of the candidates' stands on issues and their qualifications for office.

Of all the media, television bears the greatest responsibilities in campaign coverage, for it is the major source of political news for most voters. Yet there are many obstacles to thorough television coverage of campaign issues. Straightforward discussion of issues does not produce much color or excitement for TV cameras; the medium thrives on action and conflict. The short time available for the evening news further restricts any real analysis of issues and has led to the proliferation of carefully packaged media events staged by campaigns with well-placed "sound bites" that can be extracted from speeches and included in daily news coverage. Campaigns also strive for "visual bites" of telegenic symbols (such as large crowds or patriotic backgrounds) to convey their messages. Finally, TV costs play a large part in curbing ideal coverage. However, some news shows have begun to devote more time to candidate profiles, although critics complain that they still tend to be superficial. Interview shows, such as "MacNeil, Lehrer," "Nightline," and those on Cable News Network (CNN), feature in-depth questioning of the candidates.

## EQUAL-TIME PROVISIONS

The so-called equal-time rule (Section 315) of the Federal Communications Act requires a broadcaster or cablecaster that sells or gives time to a candidate to make available equal opportunities to all competing candidates for the same office, including minor-party and independent candidates. Four exceptions to the equal-opportunities requirement are permitted:

1. Regularly scheduled bona fide newscasts;
2. Bona fide news interviews;
3. Bona fide news documentaries; and
4. On-the-spot coverage of bona fide news events.

In the past, this equal-time rule discouraged coverage of major candidates by some broadcasters that did not want to include minor candidates in their broadcasts.

However, Congress suspended the equal-time provisions for the 1960 presidential and vice presidential general election campaigns. This enabled the television networks to sponsor debates between the Republican and Democratic candidates in 1960, without having to give equal time to all other presidential candidates. In 1975, the Federal Communications Commission (FCC) allowed exceptions for broadcast coverage of debates sponsored by a third party and held outside of a broadcast studio, provided they were covered in their entirety as newsworthy events. This enabled the League of Women Voters to step forward as sponsor of nationally televised debates.

Subsequently, broadcasting/cablecasting of candidate debates has been found to be covered by the fourth exception listed above, whether the event is sponsored by the broadcaster or cablecaster or by an organization such as the League of Women Voters.

## PRESIDENTIAL DEBATES

The League of Women Voters laid the groundwork for nationally televised presidential primary and general election debates, which have now become an established part of presidential campaigns. In 1976, the League of Women Voters Education Fund (LWVEF) sponsored four televised debates—three between presidential candidates Gerald Ford and Jimmy Carter and one between vice presidential candidates Walter Mondale and Robert Dole.

In 1980, after the nominations of Ronald Reagan and Jimmy Carter, John Anderson made a strong nationwide showing as a declared independent candidate, and he asked to be included in the presidential debates. Reagan and Anderson did debate, but Carter declined to participate. Subsequently, there was a debate between Carter and Reagan shortly before the election. Since this was the only face-to-face meeting of the two major candidates, this debate took on added importance.

The year 1984 was an important benchmark in the gradual institution of presidential debates; it was the third consecutive presidential election year in which the LWVEF sponsored presidential debates during primary and general election campaigns; it was the first year in which there was little or no question that debates would take place. One indication of that came when President Reagan agreed to participate, defying traditional strategic campaign judgment that debates are too risky for an incumbent who holds a strong lead in the polls.

In 1984, the LWVEF sponsored four debates at key junctures in the primary and caucus calendar. With public demand for debates increasing and relaxed FCC rules on debate sponsorship by broadcasters, other sponsors also entered the field during the primary campaign. The LWVEF was the sole sponsor of the three general election debates held in the fall of 1984—two between Ronald Reagan and Walter Mondale; one between Geraldine Ferraro and George Bush.

In 1988, the trend toward more primary debates continued. Although not all the debates were nationally televised, some candidates took part in more than 40 debates. The two major political parties formed a Commission on Presidential Debates, which offered to sponsor general election debates between the Democratic and Republican party nominees. The LWVEF, which had sponsored three of the primary debates, continued its tradition of inviting candidates for president and vice president to debate before the November election. The candidates accepted the LWVEF invitation to one presidential and one vice presidential debate. The LWVEF withdrew its invitation when the candidates' campaign staffs insisted on terms and debating conditions that the LWVEF felt benefited the candidates, not the public. The commission accepted these terms and went forward with sponsorship of three debates.

For the 1992 election, the LWVEF reaffirmed its commitment to debates by deciding to sponsor at least one presidential primary debate. CNN will cosponsor with the LWVEF a nationally and internationally televised debate the weekend before the New Hampshire primary. All four networks (ABC, CBS, CNN, and NBC) have announced plans to air a series of debates in September and October of 1992 between the Democratic and Republican presidential and vice presidential nominees.

Recently there have been questions raised about the effect of the presidential debates, and concern has been focused on three areas. First, there is criticism of the format, as some critics charge that the debates resemble joint press conferences more than true debates. For instance, there is no time for in-depth exchanges on any one particular subject, and panelists have only limited opportunities to pose follow-up questions. Second, by 1988, campaigns had become quite sophisticated in putting out the most favorable perspective on their candidates' performance (i.e., "spin control"), thus obscuring any true reaction. Finally, the media, in their increased emphasis on the "horse race" aspect of the campaign, offer instant analysis and speculation on who "won" the debate. This gives voters little time to decide independently how they viewed the debate.

Overall, however, in spite of their shortcomings, debates have played a prominent role in recent presidential elections, as they have given voters the opportunity both to hear the candidates' positions on a variety of issues and to judge their style and appearance. In 1992 debates will no doubt play a significant role once again.

## THE PRINT MEDIA

Although television has a greater capability than print to capture a large audience, news coverage would be incomplete without the wire services, daily newspapers, and news weeklies. The print media can probe the personalities of candidates and offer extensive serialized treatises on every aspect of a campaign in a way television and radio are not equipped to do. Not being subject to the technical constraints of the broadcasting trade, journalists in the print media have a greater opportunity to fully develop coverage, no matter how many candidates are out on the campaign trail.

The national wire services—Associated Press (AP) and United Press International (UPI)—provide the most widely circulated stories in the country. And what the wire reporters view as the "lead" of a story will often end up as the meat of the story in a thousand daily newspapers across the country. Because of tight deadlines and space limitations, however, these stories are generally not as analytical as the syndicated byline articles sent out by the *Los Angeles Times, Washington Post,* and *New York Times.*

## USE OF RADIO AND TV ADVERTISING BY CANDIDATES

Candidates have come to rely extensively on the broadcast media to appeal for votes. Through short TV and radio spots or elaborately prepared TV feature programs produced by their own media specialists and lasting 15 minutes to an hour, candidates hope to accentuate their own qualities and downgrade those of their opponents. Spot commercials are useful in projecting a vivid, dynamic image and are not usually intended to convey much information, though they sometimes deal with issues.

The importance of radio and television is that they give the candidates massive national exposure. Expensive as that exposure is, it takes less energy than in-person appearances, makes it possible to use travel time more efficiently, and opens up a much wider audience. Personal contact may mean more to voters, but such contact becomes impractical when there is a whole nation to reach in a short time. TV and radio ads can be replayed again and again, maximizing their usefulness.

A new form of advertising has received more attention in recent years and could play a role in the 1992 election. It is so-called narrowcasting—that is, directing specialized advertising to precisely targeted constituencies. Methods of narrowcasting include advertising on specialty cable channels that market research shows attract the desired audience and distributing videocassettes to targeted groups or individuals. (Direct mail and taped phone messages delivered via computerized telephone dialing to voters on specialized lists are two closely related, though untelevised, forms of narrowcasting.)

Use of television or radio spots peaks at the height of the campaign, usually just before election time. Many thoughtful persons fear that campaigns have become battles between advertising agencies rather than tests of candidates and issues. If much of a presidential campaign is stage-managed, they argue, voters will never see the "real" candidate or hear discussion of the "real" issues.

Television campaigning takes on an even greater significance to some critics when seen in the light of polling technology. Political advertising is increasingly based on survey research. Voters are polled as to what issues trouble them, what their attitudes are on certain issues, and how they respond to candidates. This material is then used to design a campaign that will appeal to voters' special interests or even to exploit their fears.

Media specialists defend their work on a number of grounds. They contend, on the one hand, that television is overrated, that it is only one campaign tool. On the other hand, they say that even if it is influential, political advertising serves the same purpose as commercial advertising—to inform viewers of the products available. And even short spots can be produced in such a way that they give straightforward information on a candidate's position.

Viewers know that the information is biased in favor of the product and make the necessary adjustments in their thinking. Skeptics doubt this rationale, feeling that voters do not have enough defenses against the soft sell and that, in any case, the media specialists are skillfully working to stay ahead of whatever defenses viewers have. Occasionally, the professionals are candid about the business they're in. Says one media specialist: "Damned right we don't explain. We don't educate, we motivate. That's our job. We're not teachers, we're political managers. We're trying to win."

## *Notes*

**1.** Richard Reeves, *A Ford, Not a Lincoln.*

# 9

## THE ELECTION

## The Electoral College System

The actual mechanism of electing the president and the vice president of the United States is a rather complicated process. The electoral college is one of the many compromises written into the United States Constitution in 1787. The founding fathers devised the electoral college to elect the president but they did not anticipate the emergence of national political parties or a communications network able to bring presidential candidates before the entire electorate.

Providing that the president be chosen indirectly through the "electoral college" rather than directly by the voters in November was one of the founders' hedges against "popular passion." In the beginning, the electors had very real powers to work their will. Now, their sole function is to confirm a decision made by the electorate six weeks earlier.[1]

Under the Constitution, each state is authorized to choose

electors for president and vice president, the number always being the same as the combined number of U.S. senators and representatives allotted to that state. With 100 senators and 435 representatives in the United States, plus three electors for the District of Columbia provided by the Twenty-third Amendment, the total electoral college vote is 538.[2]

Makeup and operation of the electoral college itself are tightly defined by the Constitution, but the method of choosing electors is left to the states. In the beginning many states did not provide for popular election of the presidential electors. Today, however, electors are chosen by direct popular vote in every state. When voters vote for president, they are actually voting for the electors pledged to their presidential candidate. (Electors are named by state party organizations. Serving as an elector is considered an honor, a reward for faithful service.)

With the political parties in control of presidential politics, the function of the electoral college has changed drastically. Rather than having individuals seek to become electors and then vote for whomever they please for president, the parties have turned the process upside down by arranging slates of electors, all pledged to support the candidate nominated by the party.

In the earliest days of the electoral college, quite the opposite was true. Electors cast their votes for individual candidates rather than for party slates, with the majority winner being elected president and the runner-up, vice president. This made for some bizarre situations, as in 1796 when the Federalist John Adams, with 71 votes, became president and the Democratic-Republican Thomas Jefferson, with 68, vice president—roughly equivalent in modern times to an election in which Bush and Dukakis would end up as president and vice president. In 1800 Jefferson and his running mate, Aaron Burr, each won an identical number of electoral votes, forcing the election into the House of Representatives, which resolved it in Jefferson's favor. It was to avoid any similar occurrence that the Twelfth Amendment was passed in 1804. This amendment required the electors to cast two separate ballots, one for president and the other for vice president. This is the only constitutional change that has been made in the electoral college system, other than to add three electoral votes for the District of Columbia in 1961.

Presidential and vice presidential candidates of a party run as a team. In most of the states, it is the names of the candidates rather than the names of the electors that appear on the ballot; in the other states, both candidates and electors are identified. The victor in each state is determined by counting the votes for each slate of electors; the slate receiving the most votes (the plurality, not necessarily the majority of the votes cast) is declared the winner.

To be elected to the presidency a candidate must receive an absolute majority (270) of the electoral votes cast. If no candidate receives a majority, the House of Representatives picks the winner from the top three, with each state delegation in the House casting only one vote, regardless of its size. Only two U.S. elections have been decided this way (1800 and 1824).

The vice president is elected at the same time by the same indirect winner-take-all method that chooses the president, but the electors vote separately for the two offices. If no vice presidential candidate receives a majority, the Senate picks the winner from the top two, each senator voting as an individual. The Senate has not made the choice since 1836.

## THE ELECTORAL COLLEGE PRO AND CON

The electoral college mechanism has not lacked for critics over the years. The basic objection is that the system clearly has the potential to frustrate the popular will in the selection of a president and a vice president. Because of the aggregation of electoral votes by state, it is possible that a candidate might win the most popular votes but lose in the electoral college voting. This happened in 1824 (when the election was thrown into the House), in 1876 (when there were disputed electors from several states), and in

1888. The winner-take-all system literally means that the candidate team that wins *most* of the popular votes (the plurality vote winner) in a particular state gets *all* of the electoral votes in that state, and the loser gets none, even if the loss is by a slim popular-vote margin. Thus a candidate who fails to carry a particular state receives not a single *electoral* vote in that state for the *popular* votes received. Since presidential elections are won by electoral—not popular—votes, it is the electoral vote tally that election-night viewers watch for and that tells the tale.

Another problem cited by critics is the possibility of "faithless electors" who defect from the candidate to whom they are pledged.

Most recently, in 1976, a Republican elector in the state of Washington cast his vote for Ronald Reagan instead of Gerald Ford, the Republican presidential candidate. Earlier, in 1972, a Republican elector in Virginia deserted Nixon to vote for the Libertarian party candidate. And in 1968, Nixon lost another Virginia elector, who bolted to George Wallace.

The main danger of faithless electors is that the candidate who wins the popular vote could wind up one or two votes short of a majority in the electoral college and could lose the election on a technicality. This prospect becomes more probable when there are third-party or independent candidates who could negotiate with electors before they vote.

Many see the apportioning of the electoral college votes by states as a basic flaw, because it gives each of the smaller states at least three electoral votes, even though on a straight population basis some might be entitled to only one or two.

Critics of the system also argue that the possibility that an election could be thrown into the House of Representatives is undemocratic. In such a case each state has a single vote, which gives the sparsely populated or small states equal weight with more populous states such as California or New York. The two occasions when it occurred (1800 and 1824) were marked by charges of "deals" and "corrupt bargains." In any event, giving each state one vote in the House of Representatives regardless of the number of people represented is not consistent with the widely accepted concept of one-person-one-vote. Also, one vote per state in the House of Representatives may not necessarily result in a choice that replicates the electoral vote winner in that state in November.

Those who argue in favor of retaining the present system state that there is too much uncertainty over whether any other method would be an improvement. They point out that many of the complaints about the electoral college apply just as well to the Senate and, to some extent, to the House. They fear that reform could lead to the dismantling of the federal system.

Another argument made by defenders of the electoral college is that the present method serves American democracy well by fostering a two-party system and thwarting the rise of splinter parties such as those that have plagued many European democracies. The winner-take-all system means that minor parties get few electoral votes and that a president who is the choice of the nation as a whole emerges. In the present system, splinter groups could not easily throw an election into the House. Supporters feel strongly that if the electors fail to agree on a majority president, it is in keeping with the federal system that the House of Representatives, *voting as states*, makes the selection.

Supporters also argue that the electoral college system democratically reflects population centers by giving urban areas electoral power; that is where the most votes are. Thus together, urban states come close to marshaling the requisite number of electoral votes to elect a president.

A final argument is that for the most part, the electoral college system has worked. No election in this century has been decided in the House of Representatives.[3] Further, the winner's margin of votes is usually enhanced in the electoral vote—a mathematical happening that can make the winner in a divisive and close election seem to have won more popular support than he actually did. This is thought to aid the healing of election scars and help the new president in governing.

## PROPOSALS FOR CHANGE

Discontent with the system was stimulated in the 1960s by the Wallace third-party movement and in 1980 by John Anderson's initially strong showing as an independent candidate with nationwide appeal. Also, the Supreme Court's one-person-one-vote ruling on legislative districts underscored the importance of equitable distribution of votes. A number of proposals for altering the way the president and the vice president are elected have been made. Most would require a constitutional amendment, though states can on their own change their state laws governing the way they choose electors.

One set of proposals looks toward keeping the electoral college but eliminating its winner-take-all features. This shift could be brought about by choosing most electors on a congressional district basis, with only two electors per state chosen statewide. A 1969 Maine law provides for this method, and similar legislation has been considered in several other states. Alternatively, the office of elector could be eliminated and the electoral votes of a state simply assigned to candidates on the basis of the popular vote each receives. Constitutional amendments to that effect have been introduced in Congress but none has passed. These changes might eliminate some distortion of the popular vote, but they would not answer the complaint that the people do not elect the president directly.

Former Senator Birch Bayh repeatedly introduced a constitutional amendment providing for direct election of the president and the vice president. Under the Bayh plan, candidates for president and vice president would be required to run together in each state and the District of Columbia, and voters would make their choices directly, without any intervening slate of electors. If the candidate team with the most votes received at least 40 percent of the nationwide popular vote, that pair would be declared elected; if no pair received that amount there would be a runoff election between the two top pairs.

Direct election of the president along the lines of the Bayh plan would effectively bring the one-person-one-vote principle to presidential elections. Its advocates claim that direct election would help the two-party system. Any dangers to the federal system, they argue, would be more than outweighed by the right of all the people of the United States to choose their two top elected officials directly. Opponents of direct election hold that this particular plan for change might necessitate the holding of two elections because of the runoff provision, thus making the presidential election process even more costly and drawn out than it is already. Following the defeat of the proposed amendment by the Senate in 1979, no further significant effort has been made to revive the plan.

# Election Day

A presidential election day is the consummation of the study, the planning and training, the grueling work and travel, the meeting and talking, the writing and speech making, the persuading and financing, that have been done on behalf of and by the presidential candidates. It is their day of victory or of defeat.

For many hundreds of other people, it is a long, hard day that starts for some at five in the morning when precinct workers, organized to catch voters before they leave for work, nail VOTE signs along the streets and slip reminder sheets under the doors of "their voters." In some places, the polls open at 6:00 A.M., and a full complement of poll workers, officials, watchers, and police must be on hand. Dozens of kinds of tasks, painstakingly planned, have been assigned to volunteers and regular party workers of all ages and talents. Party poll watchers, message runners, drivers to take voters to the polls, teenagers to electioneer, people to baby-sit, party workers to telephone registered voters who have not appeared at the polls, Scouts to give out "I have voted" tags—all swing into action for a long, tiring, exciting day.

Voting is supervised by election officials representing both major parties. These officials are paid a nominal fee by the local election office. Their work begins before the polls open and is far from over when the polls close. Trained to ensure proper voting procedures, they are generally responsible for overseeing the conduct of the election in the polling places. They accept absentee ballots and supervise the process of assisting voters whose physical disabilities entitle them to receive help in the voting booth. Finally, they count the votes and report the returns to the central election office, or in the case of punchcard ballots, process them in the precinct or take them to a central computer counting center.

For the candidates, election day is like an opening night for a Broadway producer. Everything that can be done has been done or is being done by campaign workers. By tradition, candidates do not campaign on election day or even make public appearances other than to vote at their own polling places. As the day ends and the time for the polls to close approaches, each candidate, like millions of other Americans, settles in front of the television set and waits for the election results to come in.

## REPORTING THE RESULTS

At one time, election nights in America were important social events. Friends and neighbors gathered at the local store or in private homes and entertained one another with food, drink, and conversation as the election results trickled in over telegraph wire or radio station. Spokespersons for candidates who were trailing in the early returns talked bravely of trends that had not yet developed and reminded supporters to "wait for the downstate returns." The leading candidates said cautiously that it was "too early to tell yet" and continued to make gloomy predictions until it was time to claim victory and congratulate the opposition on a "clean campaign." The vigil often went on until dawn.

Modern television and advances in election technology have considerably shortened the suspense period. The national networks now begin coverage of election returns before the polls close and continue until the result is known—a result that is not usually long in coming. At one time poll workers carefully counted paper ballots, inscribed the results on official sheets, and transported the ballot box to the county seat where officials would finally give the results to the media.

Today, paper ballots are rare outside rural areas, and voting machines or punchcard ballots eliminate time-consuming ballot counting. Once the polls have closed, election officials simply compile results from voting machine printer sheets or from computer tabulation of punchcard ballots. Nor do the media wait for the results to be officially reported. They hire precinct watchers to get the results at the same time election officials do and report them to the networks over special telephone lines. In that way, the television networks can flash some results on the screen soon after the polls have closed.

Television not only reports results that have been tabulated, it also projects winners on the basis of a very few returns or from "exit interviews." The procedure is the same one often used by politicians in a less extensive and less scientific way. Projections from "key" precincts—those whose returns usually closely parallel the complete returns for the state in question—are identified beforehand and information about them is fed into computers.

When returns come in, the computer is programmed to compare them with the returns of other years from the same precinct and project who the eventual winner in the state will be. If the information originally stored in the computer was incomplete or inaccurate, the predictions will, of course, be wrong. From these projections, the modern viewer often is told who has carried a state 30 minutes after the polls have closed, even though less than 5 percent of the vote may have been tabulated. With projections from exit interviews, winners can be projected well before the polls close (see "Early Projection of Election Results").

Very close elections cannot be called so quickly, and most of the network mistakes have come when the outcome was too hastily projected. On the whole, however, the projections have been accurate. There is no more "waiting for the downstate returns"; the computer has already taken such factors into account. In 1964, one network proclaimed Johnson the winner over Goldwater only a few hours after the first polls had closed. The 1968 and 1976 elections were much closer, and winners were not projected until the morning after the election. The 1980 election winner, however, was announced by all networks, and the defeated candidate had conceded before the polls had closed in the West.

In addition to reporting the results and projecting winners, the television networks also analyze the results and explain what has happened in demographic, social, and economic terms. Scholars have done this for years, of course, but not on election night. Computers are used to marshal data, enabling reporters to describe how the ethnic neighborhoods voted in Chicago, how a candidate is doing in farm areas, and so forth. The meaning of the election will be studied for years, but television, as usual, reports it first. In short, what it once took weeks to find out about the outcome of the election, the viewer now knows before retiring on election night.

# Early Projection of Election Results

Techniques such as exit polls and sample precinct analysis combined with modern computer technology have made possible the early projection of winners by networks and news services.

Following the 1980 election when Ronald Reagan was projected winner on all three networks before the polls closed in the West *and* when President Carter conceded the election at 9:45 P.M. EST, hearings were held in Congress to address the growing controversy over such practices. Critics charged that the networks' rush to project a winner overlooked the effect by a less-than-expected turnout in the West and on close, nonpresidential races that could be affected by a less-than-expected turnout. Polls taken in the months following the 1980 election showed that many citizens in all parts of the country were angered and alarmed by the growing practice of predicting winners on the basis of exit polls and sample precinct analysis.

Some legislators and network representatives alike have called for a variety of legislative proposals to remedy the early projection situation, such as uniform poll closing time or 24-hour voting. But many fear such cures would be worse than the problem because of their effects on voting patterns or on the costs of administering elections. Others question what will happen if the media cease to simply report events but use techniques that might actually change the outcome of elections.

In spite of the problems caused by early projections, each of the national TV networks continues to maintain that their First Amendment rights would be abridged by any form of restraint on their ability to project winners.

# The Final Stages

When the final election results are in, the entire country knows who the next president and vice president will be, but the outcome must still be formalized. In December, the electors who were chosen in November travel to their respective state capitals for the brief ceremony of assembling to cast their official electoral votes, signing necessary documents, and posing for pictures. Then they go home. Their brief moment of glory is soon over as state officials certify their results and transmit their official ballots to Washington.

When Congress convenes in January, the electoral vote documents from all 50 states and the District of Columbia are opened before a joint session of the two houses and the official results announced. In nearly every American presidential election, this is a formality only. The election winner is already being referred to as the president-elect and has been preparing for weeks to assume office.

Presidential transitions are not easy for either the person leaving office or the person coming into it. A "lame duck" president must carry on with presidential duties even while carrying less weight than before the election in domestic, political, and international circles. It is considered bad form for the president-elect to offer policy advice during the transitional period; an outgoing president does not usually seek it.

The atmosphere of suspended animation that characterizes a presidential transition could cause problems if a severe crisis were to arise. For example, what should be the attitude of a president-elect if a nuclear confrontation with a foreign power were to develop in December? No one knows the answer because the country has been spared any such development, but the general attitude of presidents-elect has been that the country has only one president at a time, that the powers of the presidency do not come in stages but all at once—today, an ordinary citizen; tomorrow, the most important elected official in the world.

At noon on January 20 following a presidential election, the term of the preceding president ends and that of the incoming president begins.[4] At a formal inauguration ceremony, the Chief Justice of the United States Supreme Court[5] swears in the president and the vice president before members of Congress, government dignitaries, representatives of foreign governments, and a host of important well-wishers. The new chief executive makes an inaugural address and a parade usually follows. A new president has begun the duties of office. The election process has concluded and a new election period now begins.

# *Notes*

**1.** An "elector" is simply a person who elects someone else. The term *college* refers to a decision-making group such as the College of Cardinals, which elects the pope.

2. For comprehensive discussions of the development and operation of the electoral college system—its pros and cons and possible reforms—see League of Women Voters of the United States, *Who Should Elect the President?;* Joseph Gorman, *Elections: Electoral College Reform;* and Lawrence D. Longley and Alan G. Brown, *The Politics of the Electoral College.*

3. In 1876, the House decided which of two disputed sets of electoral votes to accept from certain southern states.

4. Before the adoption in 1933 of the Twentieth Amendment, presidents were inaugurated on March 4.

5. In an emergency, a president may take the oath of office before any official authorized to administer oaths, even a notary public. After the assassination of President John F. Kennedy in 1963, Lyndon Johnson was sworn in as president by Federal Judge Sarah Hughes in the presidential plane at the Dallas airport.

# AFTERWORD

This book has been written to explain the presidential nomination and election process. Its premise is the value of individual participation at all stages of the operation.

The long and arduous path for choosing the president puts the presidential hopefuls under scrutiny by giving you an opportunity to evaluate their performance: as *leaders*—their ability to inspire trust; as *administrators*—their organizational skills; and as *individuals*—their honesty, competence, sensitivity, and integrity.

Their campaign organizations may be viewed as mini-White Houses—precursors of an administration-to-be. If you look closely you can see how they operate as money managers, how realistic their proposals are, how they deal with the press, how much personal contact they try to develop with the public, and how responsive they are to citizen concerns.

And you can do more than just watch. The thing to do is to start asking questions—find out who and where the party leaders are. Call your local party headquarters, volunteer your services, ask about times and places of meetings, ask your neighbors about what's what politically in your area, call the League of Women Voters. The qualification necessary for political involvement is interest. You *can* make a difference.

No presidential election has ever been, or is likely to be, decided by one vote, but it is true that more than once a shift of relatively few votes in the right states would have changed the outcome under the electoral college system. The most drastic case in recent years was the 1960 election—when John Kennedy won the presidential election by an average of only one vote per precinct.

The closer the balance between the parties in a state, the more important is your single vote, and with a real two-party system throughout the country, the competition for each vote is growing in practically every state. Even if the election outcome seems almost a foregone conclusion, a vote cast in a losing cause is not a wasted vote. It can be politically worthwhile as a way to build or retain strength for the future. If, for instance, every southern Republican had stopped voting during the years of Democratic domination of the South, the modern Republican party could never have developed as it has in recent years.

The legitimacy of the chief executive's leadership is affected by who, to begin with, elects the president. And if only a small fraction of the public turns out to vote the individual into office, our democratic system will fall short of its potential for the people to realize their power. Changes in all aspects of our political system—some of which have been described in this book—mean that in 1992 American government rests far more than ever before in our history on individual participation, on *your* participation, at every stage in the election process.

# APPENDIX A: PROVISIONS IN THE U.S. CONSTITUTION RELATING TO THE PRESIDENCY

## UNITED STATES CONSTITUTION

ARTICLE II—The President

Section 1. The executive power shall be vested in a President of the United States of America. He shall hold his office during the term of four years, and, together with the Vice President, chosen for the same term, be elected, as follows.

Each State shall appoint, in such manner as the legislature thereof may direct, a number of electors, equal to the whole number of Senators and Representatives to which the State may be entitled in the Congress: but no Senator or Representative, or person holding an office of trust or profit under the United States, shall be appointed an elector. . . .

The Congress may determine the time of choosing the electors, and the day on which they shall give their votes; which day shall be the same throughout the United States.

AMENDMENT XII—Presidential Electors

The electors shall meet in their respective States, and vote by ballot for President and Vice President, one of whom, at least, shall not be an inhabitant of the same State with themselves; they shall name in their ballots the person voted for as President and in distinct ballots the person voted for as Vice President, and they shall make distinct lists of all persons voted for as President, and of all persons voted for as Vice President, and of the number of votes for each, which lists they shall sign and certify, and transmit sealed to the seat of the government of the United States, directed to the President of the Senate;—The President of the Senate shall, in the presence of the Senate and House of Representatives, open all the certificates and the votes shall then be counted;—The person having the greatest number of votes for President, shall be the President, if such number be a majority of the whole number of electors appointed; and if no person have such majority, then from the persons having the highest numbers not exceeding three on the list of those voted for as President, the House of Representatives shall choose immediately, by ballot, the President. But in choosing the President, the votes shall be taken by States, the representation from each State having one vote; a quorum for this purpose shall consist of a member or members from two-thirds of the States, and a majority of all the States shall be necessary to a choice. And if the House of Representatives shall not choose a President whenever the right of choice shall devolve upon them, before the fourth day of March[1] next following, then the Vice President shall act as President, as in the case of the death or other constitutional disability of the President.[2]—The person having the greatest number of votes as Vice President, shall be the Vice President, if such number be a majority of the whole number of electors appointed, and if no person have a majority, then from the two highest numbers on the list, the Senate shall choose the Vice President; a quorum for the purpose shall consist of two-thirds of the whole number of Senators, and a majority of the whole number shall be necessary to a choice. But no person constitutionally ineligible to the office of President shall be eligible to that of Vice President of the United States. (Ratified in 1804)

AMENDMENT XX—Lame-Duck Amendment

Section 3. If, at the time fixed for the beginning of the term of the President, the President elect shall have died, the Vice President elect shall become President. If a President shall not have been chosen before the time fixed for the beginning of his term, or if the President elect shall have failed to qualify, then the Vice President elect shall act as President until a President shall have qualified; and the Congress may by law provide for the case wherein neither a President elect nor a Vice President elect shall have qualified, declaring who shall then act as President, or the manner in which one who is to act shall be selected, and such person shall act accordingly until a President or Vice President shall have qualified.

Section 4. The Congress may by law provide for the case of the death of any of the persons from whom the House of Representatives may choose a President whenever the right of choice shall have devolved upon them, and for the case of the death of any of the persons from whom the Senate may choose a Vice President whenever the right of choice shall have devolved upon them. (Ratified in 1933)

## Notes

1. By the Twentieth Amendment, adopted in 1933, the term of the president is to begin on January 20.
2. Under the Twentieth Amendment, Section 3, in case a president is not chosen before the final time fixed for the beginning of his term, the vice president elect shall act as president until a president shall have qualified.

# APPENDIX B:
# THE PRESIDENTIAL OFFICE

## QUALIFICATIONS FOR OFFICE

Natural-born citizen; at least 35 years old; 14 years or more a resident within the United States.

U.S. CONSTITUTION, ARTICLE II
Section 1.... No person except a natural born citizen, or a citizen of the United States, at the time of the adoption of this Constitution, shall be eligible to the office of President; neither shall any person be eligible to that office who shall not have attained to the age of thirty-five years, and been fourteen years a resident within the United States....

## TERM OF OFFICE

Four years, beginning on January 20 of the year following election; no more than two terms or ten years.

U.S. CONSTITUTION, AMENDMENT XX
Section 1. The terms of the President and Vice President shall end at noon on the 20th day of January, and the terms of Senators and Representatives at noon on the 3d day of January, of the years in which such terms would have ended if this article had not been ratified; and the terms of their successors shall then begin.

No more than two terms or ten years.

U.S. CONSTITUTION, AMENDMENT XXII
Section 1. No person shall be elected to the office of the President more than twice, and no person who has held the office of President, or acted as President, for more than two years of a term to which some other person was elected President shall be elected to the office of the President more than once. But this article shall not apply to any person holding the office of President when this article was proposed by the Congress, and shall not prevent any person who may be holding the office of President, or acting as President, during the term within which this article becomes operative from holding the office of President or acting as President during the remainder of such term. (Ratified in 1951)

## PRESIDENTIAL OATH OF OFFICE

U.S. CONSTITUTION, ARTICLE II
Section 1. . . . Before he enter on the execution of his office, he shall take the following oath or affirmation:—"I do solemnly swear (or affirm) that I will faithfully execute the office of President of the United States, and will to the best of my ability, preserve, protect and defend the Constitution of the United States."

## PRESIDENTIAL REMUNERATION

U.S. CONSTITUTION, ARTICLE II
Section 1. . . . The President shall, at stated times, receive for his

services, a compensation, which shall neither be increased nor diminished during the period for which he shall have been elected, and he shall not receive within that period any other emolument from the United States, or any of them.

# DUTIES AND POWERS OF THE PRESIDENT

U.S. CONSTITUTION, ARTICLE II
Section 2. The President shall be Commander in Chief of the Army and Navy of the United States, and of the militia of the several States, when called into the actual service of the United States; he may require the opinion, in writing, of the principal officer in each of the executive departments, upon any subject relating to the duties of their respective offices, and he shall have power to grant reprieves and pardons for offenses against the United States, except in cases of impeachment.

He shall have power, by and with the advice and consent of the Senate, to make treaties, provided two-thirds of the Senators present concur; and he shall nominate, and by and with the advice and consent of the Senate, shall appoint ambassadors, other public ministers and consuls, Judges of the Supreme Court, and all other officers of the United States, whose appointments are not herein otherwise provided for, and which shall be established by law: but the Congress may by law vest the appointment of such inferior officers, as they think proper, in the President alone, in the courts of law, or in the heads of departments. . . .

Section 3. He shall from time to time give to the Congress information of the State of the Union, and recommend to their consideration such measures as he shall judge necessary and expedient; he may, on extraordinary occasions, convene both Houses, or either of them, and in case of disagreement between them, with respect to the time of adjournment, he may adjourn them to such time as he shall think proper; he shall receive ambassadors and other public ministers; he shall take care that the laws be faithfully executed, and shall commission all the officers of the United States.

Section 4. The President, Vice President, and all civil officers of the United States, shall be removed from office on impeachment for, and conviction of, treason, bribery, or other high crimes and misdemeanors.

## SUCCESSION TO THE PRESIDENCY

U.S. CONSTITUTION, AMENDMENT XXV

Section 1. In case of the removal of the President from office or of his death or resignation, the Vice President shall become President.

Section 2. Whenever there is a vacancy in the office of the Vice President, the President shall nominate a Vice President who shall take office upon confirmation by a majority vote of both Houses of Congress.

Section 3. Whenever the President transmits to the President pro tempore of the Senate and the Speaker of the House of Representatives his written declaration that he is unable to discharge the powers and duties of his office, and until he transmits to them a written declaration to the contrary, such powers and duties shall be discharged by the Vice President as Acting President.

Section 4. Whenever the Vice President and a majority of either the principal officers of the executive departments or of such other body as Congress may by law provide, transmit to the President pro tempore of the Senate and the Speaker of the House of Representatives their written declaration that the President is unable to discharge the powers and duties of his office, the Vice President shall immediately assume the powers and duties of the office as Acting President.

Thereafter, when the President transmits to the President pro tempore of the Senate and the Speaker of the House of Representatives his written declaration that no inability exists, he shall resume the powers and duties of his office unless the Vice President and a majority of either the principal officers of the executive department or of such other body as Congress may by law provide, transmit within four days to the President pro tempore of the Senate and the Speaker of the House of Representatives their written declaration that the President is unable to discharge the powers and duties of his office. Thereupon Congress shall decide the issue, assembling within forty-eight hours for that purpose if not in session. If the Congress, within twenty-one days after receipt of the latter written declaration, or, if Congress is not in session, within twenty-one days after Congress is required to assemble, determines by two-thirds vote of both Houses that the President is unable to discharge the powers and duties of his office, the Vice President shall continue to discharge the same as Acting President; otherwise, the President shall resume the powers and duties of his office. (Ratified in 1967)

| President | Died in | Was Succeeded by Vice President |
|---|---|---|
| W. H. Harrison | 1841 | John Tyler |
| Zachary Taylor | 1850 | Millard Fillmore |
| Abraham Lincoln | 1865 | Andrew Johnson |
| James A. Garfield | 1881 | Chester A. Arthur |
| William McKinley | 1901 | Theodore Roosevelt |
| Warren G. Harding | 1923 | Calvin Coolidge |
| Franklin D. Roosevelt | 1945 | Harry S. Truman |
| John F. Kennedy | 1963 | Lyndon B. Johnson |
| | **Resigned in** | |
| Richard M. Nixon | 1974 | Gerald R. Ford |

Presidential succession has never yet gone beyond the vice presidency. By the Presidential Succession Act of 1947, as amended, the line of succession to the presidency, first to last, is:

Vice President
Speaker of the House
President Pro Tempore of the Senate
Secretary of State
Secretary of the Treasury
Secretary of Defense
Attorney General
Secretary of the Interior
Secretary of Agriculture
Secretary of Commerce
Secretary of Labor
Secretary of Health and Human Services
Secretary of Housing and Urban Development
Secretary of Transportation
Secretary of Energy
Secretary of Education

## VACANCIES IN THE VICE PRESIDENCY

The office of the vice president has been vacant 18 times, for a total of more than 37 years. Nine vice presidents left the office vacant when they went to the White House to fill a presidential vacancy. Seven vice presidents died in office:

| Vice President | Died in | Under President |
| --- | --- | --- |
| George Clinton | 1812 | James Madison (1st term) |
| Elbridge Gerry | 1814 | James Madison (2nd term) |
| William R. King | 1853 | Franklin Pierce |
| Henry Wilson | 1875 | Ulysses S. Grant |
| Thomas A. Hendricks | 1885 | Grover Cleveland |
| Garret A. Hobart | 1899 | William McKinley |
| James S. Sherman | 1912 | William H. Taft |

Two vice presidents resigned: John C. Calhoun resigned in 1832 as vice president under Andrew Jackson to become a U.S. senator. He had been vice president since 1825, under both Jackson and John Quincy Adams. Spiro Agnew resigned in 1973 as vice president under Richard Nixon shortly before pleading "no contest" to charges of income tax evasion.

# APPENDIX C: CONSTITUTIONAL AMENDMENTS EXPANDING THE SUFFRAGE

AMENDMENT XV
Section 1. The right of citizens of the United States to vote shall not be denied or abridged by the United States or by any State on account of race, color, or previous condition of servitude. (Ratified in 1870)

AMENDMENT XVII
Section 1. The Senate of the United States shall be composed of two Senators from each State, elected by the people thereof, for six years; and each Senator shall have one vote. The electors in each State shall have the qualifications requisite for electors of the most numerous branch of the State legislatures. (Ratified in 1913)

AMENDMENT XIX
Section 1. The right of citizens of the United States to vote shall

not be denied or abridged by the United States or by any State on account of sex. (Ratified in 1920)

## AMENDMENT XXIII

Section 1. The District constituting the seat of Government of the United States shall appoint in such manner as the Congress may direct:

A number of electors of President and Vice President equal to the whole number of Senators and Representatives in Congress to which the District would be entitled if it were a State, but in no event more than the least populous State; they shall be in addition to those appointed by the States, but they shall be considered, for the purposes of the election of President and Vice President, to be electors appointed by a State; and they shall meet in the District and perform such duties as provided by the twelfth article of amendment. (Ratified in 1961)

## AMENDMENT XXIV

Section 1. The right of citizens of the United States to vote in any primary or other election for President or Vice President, for electors for President or Vice President, or for Senator or Representative in Congress, shall not be denied or abridged by the United States or any State by reason of failure to pay any poll tax or other tax. (Ratified in 1964)

## AMENDMENT XXVI

Section 1. The right of citizens of the United States who are eighteen years of age or older, to vote shall not be denied or abridged by the United States or by any State on account of age. (Ratified in 1971)

# APPENDIX D: EVOLUTION OF THE PRESIDENTIAL NOMINATION PROCESS

**1789–1792**   Early nonpartisan system. George Washington was twice elected unanimously with no formal nomination.

**1796**   Beginning of party control of political nominations generally and legislative caucus method of making presidential nominations. John Adams is last Federalist to be elected.

**1800–1820**   Federalist and Democratic-Republican (Jeffersonian) nominees, chosen in legislative caucus, battle regularly in elections.

**1820–1824**   "Era of Good Feeling." James Monroe renominated by Democratic-Republicans by common consent with no formal action and wins in electoral college 231 to 1.

**1824** Andrew Jackson defies legislative caucus and wins nomination of Tennessee legislature. Fails in election when presidential choice thrown into House of Representatives and John Quincy Adams wins in "corrupt bargain."

**1828** Andrew Jackson is again nominated by Tennessee legislature and wins election, signaling new era by gaining power as result of well-organized popular movement. Caucus method of nomination now in disrepute.

**1831** First national party convention in modern sense held in Baltimore by Anti-Masonic party. William Wirt nominated, but party fails to survive long.

**1832** First Democratic national convention held in May in Baltimore as Jacksonian revolution continues. Andrew Jackson (for president) and Martin Van Buren (for vice president) nominated and elected.

**1839** With convention method of nomination now becoming established, Whigs hold their first national convention. They elect two presidents but cannot survive the slavery turmoil.

**1856** First Republican national convention held in June in Philadelphia as new major party emerges. John Fremont is first presidential candidate.

**1860** Republicans nominate first winning presidential candidate in Abraham Lincoln.

**1860–1908** Democratic and Republican national conventions dominate presidential nominations except for brief threat from Populists in 1890s.

**1910** Oregon passes first presidential primary law as charges of bossism in conventions grow. Other states follow.

**1912**  First presidential election year with presidential primaries. New method allows Theodore Roosevelt to demonstrate popular support, but William Taft wins nomination.

**1972**  Reforms in the Republican and Democratic parties.

**1976**  Thirty-one states held primaries.

**1980**  Thirty-five states held primaries.

**1992**  Thirty-four states will hold primaries.

# APPENDIX E:
# ELECTORAL VOTES BY STATE

## Total: 538   Needed to Win: 270

|  | 1992 | 1984 | 1980 | CHANGE (1984–92) |
|---|---|---|---|---|
| California | 54 | 47 | 45 | +7 |
| New York | 33 | 36 | 41 | -3 |
| Texas | 32 | 29 | 26 | +3 |
| Pennsylvania | 23 | 25 | 27 | -2 |
| Illinois | 22 | 24 | 26 | -2 |
| Ohio | 21 | 23 | 25 | -2 |
| Florida | 25 | 21 | 17 | +4 |
| Michigan | 18 | 20 | 21 | -2 |
| New Jersey | 15 | 16 | 17 | -1 |
| Massachusetts | 12 | 13 | 14 | -1 |
| North Carolina | 14 | 13 | 13 | +1 |
| Georgia | 13 | 12 | 12 | +1 |
| Indiana | 12 | 12 | 13 | - |
| Virginia | 13 | 12 | 12 | +1 |
| Missouri | 11 | 11 | 12 | - |

| | | | |
|---|---|---|---|
| Tennessee | 11 | 11 | 10 | - |
| Wisconsin | 11 | 11 | 11 | - |
| Louisiana | 9 | 10 | 10 | -1 |
| Maryland | 10 | 10 | 10 | - |
| Minnesota | 10 | 10 | 10 | - |
| Washington | 11 | 10 | 9 | +1 |
| Alabama | 9 | 9 | 9 | - |
| Kentucky | 8 | 9 | 9 | -1 |
| Colorado | 8 | 8 | 7 | - |
| Connecticut | 8 | 8 | 8 | - |
| Iowa | 7 | 8 | 8 | -1 |
| Oklahoma | 8 | 8 | 8 | - |
| South Carolina | 8 | 8 | 8 | - |
| Arizona | 8 | 7 | 6 | +1 |
| Kansas | 6 | 7 | 7 | -1 |
| Mississippi | 7 | 7 | 7 | - |
| Oregon | 7 | 7 | 6 | - |
| Arkansas | 6 | 6 | 6 | - |
| West Virginia | 5 | 6 | 6 | -1 |
| Nebraska | 5 | 5 | 5 | - |
| New Mexico | 5 | 5 | 4 | - |
| Utah | 5 | 5 | 4 | - |
| Hawaii | 4 | 4 | 4 | - |
| Idaho | 4 | 4 | 4 | - |
| Maine | 4 | 4 | 4 | - |
| Montana | 3 | 4 | 4 | -1 |
| Nevada | 4 | 4 | 3 | - |
| New Hampshire | 4 | 4 | 4 | - |
| Rhode Island | 4 | 4 | 4 | - |
| Alaska | 3 | 3 | 3 | - |
| Delaware | 3 | 3 | 3 | - |
| District of Columbia | 3 | 3 | 3 | - |
| North Dakota | 3 | 3 | 3 | - |
| South Dakota | 3 | 3 | 3 | - |
| Vermont | 3 | 3 | 3 | - |
| Wyoming | 3 | 3 | 3 | - |

# APPENDIX F: CURRENT LAWS FOR CAMPAIGN FINANCE

Since Congress started legislating the financing of national elections, a number of provisions have come and gone. The provisions no longer on the books have either been superseded by congressional action or been declared unconstitutional by the Supreme Court.

The following provisions regulating presidential campaigns, listed in order of the progress of the nomination and general election campaigns, are still on the books. The provisions are followed by a reference to the appropriate legislation or ruling. When one year's amendments superseded previous law, both citations are listed.

- *Federal regulation.* The Federal Election Commission (FEC) is the federal agency responsible for enforcement of campaign laws (Federal Election Campaign Act of 1971 [FECA], amendments of 1976).
- *Disclosure.* Presidential candidates must file regular reports listing campaign contributions and expenditures (1971).

Donors of $200 or more must be listed on the reports (1971, 1979 amendments). Any organization spending more than $5,000 on campaigns must establish formal political committees (FECA 1971, 1979). Those reports go to the FEC (1974, 1976 amendments). Candidates must establish a single organization for their campaigns (1974). The name of the candidate must be listed on campaign materials (1979).

- *Expenses of local party organizations.* Certain expenses, such as get-out-the-vote drives and voter education activities, do not have to be reported (1979). Up to $1,000 in voluntary services, such as lending a home for meetings and lodging, do not have to be reported as contributions (1979).
- *Independent spending.* Independent spending of $250 or more must be reported to the FEC (1971, 1979). Organizations without formal ties to campaign organizations do not have to adhere to spending limitations (1974).
- *"Lowest-unit" rule.* Broadcasters can charge campaigns only as much as they charge other advertising clients for spot commercials (1971).
- *Political action committees (PACs).* Corporations and labor unions may establish separate units to promote political ends and not be in violation of federal prohibitions on direct contributions (1971).
- *Equal time.* Broadcasters selling or giving time to a federal candidate must provide equal time to the candidate's campaign opponents (Section 315 of the Federal Communications Act). Typically, this law gives spokespersons for both parties a chance to respond to the remarks of the other. After a State of the Union address, for example, a representative of the other party delivers a statement. Hollywood movies featuring Ronald Reagan were not permitted to be aired on television during his 1976, 1980, and 1984 campaigns because of this provision.
- *Taxpayer checkoff.* Citizens may indicate on their tax forms that they would like $1 ($2 for joint filings) of their tax

money to be put into the Presidential Election Campaign Fund. This fund has been used to help finance nomination and general election campaigns (1971).

- *Matching funds during primaries.* Candidates may receive federal matching funds if they raise at least $100,000 in 20 or more states. Each of those states must contribute a total of $5,000 to the candidate in individual donations of $250 or less (1974).

- *Limits on contributions.* Citizens may contribute only $1,000 to each primary or general election campaign, a total of $25,000 to federal candidates overall, and $20,000 to committees of national parties (1976). Candidates may spend only $50,000 of their own or their family's money on their campaigns if they accept federal funding (1971, 1976).

- *Multicandidate committees.* Multicandidate committees—most commonly PACs—may contribute only $5,000 per candidate and $15,000 to committees of the national parties (1976).

- *Federal funding of national conventions.* The parties receive $3 million each for their summer conventions (1974, 1979).

- *Spending limits.* Candidates receiving federal matching funds may spend limited amounts during the nomination season and other limited amounts in each of the states (state limits are determined by population). The limit in 1976, the first year this provision was in effect, was $10 million; the limit has been adjusted to account for inflation.

- *Federal funding of general election campaigns.* The federal government offers the nominee of the major parties equal sums of money for the general election campaign. Candidates who accept the money may not raise or use additional campaign funds. The figure was $17 million in 1976; the amount has been adjusted each election year according to the inflation rate (1974).

*Source:* Michael Nelson, ed., *Congressional Quarterly's Guide to the Presidency,* Washington, DC: Congressional Quarterly, Inc., 1989.

# APPENDIX G: PROTECTION OF CANDIDATES FOR THE PRESIDENCY

The assassination of President William McKinley in 1901 provided the impetus for initiating Secret Service protection of presidents. But presidential aspirants were not given this security option until the assassination of Senator Robert F. Kennedy 67 years later, when President Johnson issued an executive order calling for protection of all announced major candidates for the presidency. This later became law, with the provision that candidates could decline protection.

A five-person advisory committee determines whether prospective candidates meet the criteria for protection. To qualify, a candidate must:

- Be a declared candidate;
- Have received financial contributions and be likely to qualify for federal matching funds; and
- Conduct an active campaign.

There are, however, exceptions to these criteria. In 1979 Senator Edward Kennedy was given Secret Service protection even though he had not formally declared his candidacy for president.

# APPENDIX H: SIGNIFICANT PRESIDENTIAL ELECTIONS

With the electoral college system, it is possible for a candidate to be elected by a majority of the electoral votes, even though he may not have had a majority of the popular votes throughout the nation (majority means one more than half).

Elected without popular majorities, but with popular pluralities (the most votes) in a field of more than two candidates were:[1]

| | |
|---|---|
| James K. Polk in 1844 | Grover Cleveland in 1892 |
| Zachary Taylor in 1848 | Woodrow Wilson in 1912 |
| James Buchanan in 1856 | Woodrow Wilson in 1916 |
| Abraham Lincoln in 1860 | Harry S. Truman in 1948 |
| James A. Garfield in 1880 | John F. Kennedy in 1960 |
| Grover Cleveland in 1884 | Richard M. Nixon in 1968 |

Elected with neither majorities nor pluralities of *popular* votes were:

- John Quincy Adams in 1824 (election decided by House of Representatives)
- Rutherford B. Hayes in 1876 (election decided by congressional electoral commission)
- Benjamin Harrison in 1888 (received majority of *electoral* vote)

The closest presidential election in 76 years occurred in 1960. Kennedy's official plurality after recounts was 118,263 votes in a record 68 million-plus votes cast. His plurality percentage was the thinnest margin—less than one-half of 1 percent. Electoral votes cast were: 303 for Kennedy; 219 for Nixon; 15 for Senator Harry F. Byrd of Virginia (from electors in Mississippi, Alabama, and Oklahoma). Kennedy won seven states (Delaware, Hawaii, Illinois, Minnesota, Missouri, New Jersey, New Mexico) by less than 1 percent of the popular vote in each.

These seven states had a total of 77 electoral votes—much more than enough to swing the election to him. Five additional states (Michigan, Nevada, Pennsylvania, South Carolina, Texas) gave Kennedy their electoral votes (87) with a less than 2 percent plurality of popular vote. Altogether these 12 states, in which Kennedy won with a less than 2 percent popular plurality, had a total electoral vote of 164, far more than half the electoral votes Kennedy received to win the election.

# *Notes*

1. Examples of third-party presidential nominees in this century who have received elctoral votes: in 1912, Theodore Roosevelt, Progressive (Bull Moose) party—88 electoral votes; in 1924, Robert M. La Follette, Sr., Progressive—13 electoral votes; in 1948, J. Strom Thurmond, States' Rights party (Dixiecrat)—39 electoral votes; in 1968, George C. Wallace, American Independent party—46 electoral votes.

# BIBLIOGRAPHY

Alexander, Herbert E. "Communications and Politics: The Media and the Message." *Law and Contemporary Problems*. Duke University School of Law, Durham, N.C., Spring 1971.

_____*Financing the 1984 Election*. Lexington, Mass.: Lexington Books, 1983.

American Political Dictionary, 8th ed. New York: Holt, Rinehart & Winston, 1989.

Asher, Herbert B. *Presidential Elections and American Politics*, 3d ed. Homewood, Ill.: Dorsey Press, 1984.

Barber, James D., ed. *Choosing the President*. Englewood Cliffs, N.J.: Prentice-Hall, 1974.

Barone, Michael, and Grant Ujifusa. *The Almanac of American Politics, 1992*, Washington, DC: National Journal, 1991.

Baxter, Sandra, and Marjorie Lansing. *Women and Politics: The Visible Majority*. Ann Arbor: University of Michigan Press, 1983.

Broder, James S. "Conventions Losing Their Surprises." *Sacramento Bee*. Washington Post Writers Group, September 4, 1991.

Campbell, Angus, et al. *The American Voter*. New York: John Wiley & Sons, 1960.

Cantor, Joseph E. *Political Action Committees: Their Evolution and Growth and Their Implications for the Political System*. Washington, D.C.: Congressional Research Service, Library of Congress, 1981; rev. ed., 1982.

*Citizens and Politics: A View from Main Street America*. Prepared for the Kettering Foundation by the Harwood Group. The Kettering Foundation, 1991.

Crittenden, John A. *Parties and Elections in the United States*. Englewood Cliffs, N.J.: Prentice-Hall, 1982.

*CQ Guide to Current American Government,* Fall 1991 Guide. Washington, D.C.: Congressional Quarterly, Inc., 1991.

"Debates Take Shape." *Congressional Quarterly Weekly Report*, September 17, 1988, p. 2601.

Democratic Party of the U.S. *Delegate Selection Rules for the 1992 Democratic Convention*. Washington, D.C., 1991.

Gilligan, Jane, ed. *Elections '88*. Washington, D.C.: Congressional Quarterly Inc., 1988.

Gorman, Joseph. *Elections: Electoral College Reform*. Washington, D.C.: Congressional Research Service, Library of Congress, January 1976.

_____*Elections: Presidential Primaries*. Washington, D.C.: Congressional Research Service, Library of Congress, Issue Brief, continually revised.

Heard, Alexander. *Made in America: Improving the Nomination and Election of Presidents*. New York: HarperCollins Publishers, 1991.

Hill, David B., and Norman R. Luttbeg. *Trends in American Electoral Behavior*. 2d ed. Itasca, Ill.: F.E. Peacock Publishers, 1983.

Hoffman, Mark S., ed. *The World Almanac and Book of Facts 1990*. New York: Pharos Books, 1990.

Johnson, Walter. *How We Drafted Adlai Stevenson*. New York: Alfred A. Knopf, 1955.

Kelley, Stanley. *Interpreting Elections*. Princeton, N.J.: Princeton University Press, 1983.

Key, V.O., Jr. *Politics, Parties and Pressure Groups*, 5th ed. New York: Thomas Y. Crowell, 1964.

Lawrence, Christine C., ed. *Congressional Quarterly Almanac: 100th Congress 2nd Session . . . 1988*, vol. 44. Washington, D.C.: Congressional Quarterly Inc., 1989.

_____*Congressional Quarterly Almanac: 101st Congress 1st Session . . . 1989*, Volume 45. Washington, D.C.: Congressional Quarterly Inc., 1990.

League of Women Voters Education Fund. *Choosing the President, 1984: A Complete Guide to Understanding the Presidential Election Process*. New York: Schocken Books, 1984.

League of Women Voters Education Fund. *Election '76: Issues Not Images*. Washington, D.C., 1976.

League of Women Voters of the United States. *Who Should Elect the President?* Washington, D.C., 1969.

Longley, Lawrence D., and Alan G. Brown. *The Politics of the Electoral College*. New Haven, Conn.: Yale University Press, 1972.

Magleby, David B. and Candice J. Nelson. *The Money Chase: Congressional Campaign Finance Reform*. Washington, D.C.: The Brookings Institution, 1990.

Mandel, Ruth B. *In the Running: The New Woman Candidate*. New Haven, Conn.: Ticknor & Fields, 1981.

Nelson, Michael, ed. *Congressional Quarterly's Guide to the Presidency*. Washington, D.C.: Congressional Quarterly Inc., 1989.

_____*The Elections of 1988*. Washington, D.C.: CQ Press, 1989.

Nugent, Margaret L., and John R. Johannes, eds. *Money, Elections, and Democracy: Reforming Congressional Campaign Finance*. Boulder, Colo.: Westview Press, Inc., 1990.

Parris, Judith N. *The Convention Problem: Issues in Reform of Presidential Nominating Procedures*. Washington, D.C.: Brookings Institution, 1972.

Polsby, Nelson W. *Presidential Elections*. New York: Scribner, 1980.

Pomper, Gerald M., et al. *The Election of 1988—Reports and Interpretations*. Chatham, N. J.: Chatham House Publishers, Inc., 1989.

Pomper, Gerald M. *Voter's Choice: Varieties of American Electoral Behavior*. New York: Harper & Row, 1975.

Reeves, Richard. *A Ford, Not a Lincoln: The Decline of American Leadership*. New York: Harcourt Brace Jovanovich, 1975.

Reichley, A. James, ed. *Elections American Style*. Washington, D.C.: The Brookings Institution, 1987.

Republican National Committee. *How a President Is Nominated and Selected*. Washington, D.C., 1991.

Ripon Society and Clifford W. Brown, Jr. *Jaws of Victory*. Boston: Little, Brown, 1974.

Rosenstone, Steven J. *Forecasting Presidential Elections*. New Haven, Conn.: Yale University Press, 1983.

Sabato, Larry J. *Paying for Elections: The Campaign Finance Thicket*. New York: Priority Press Publications, 1989.

Salmore, Barbara G., and Stephen A. Salmore. *Candidates, Parties, and Campaigns: Electoral Politics in America*, 2d ed. Washington, D.C.: CQ Press, 1989.

Scammon, Richard M. *America Votes*. America Votes Series, vol. 10. Washington, D.C.: Congressional Quarterly, Inc., continually revised.

Stanley, Harold W., and Richard G. Niemi. *Vital Statistics on American Politics*. 2d and 3d eds. Washington, D.C.: CQ Press, 1990.

Watson, Richard A. *The Presidential Contest*, 3d ed. Washington, D.C.: CQ Press, 1988.

Wayne, Stephen J. *The Road to the White House*. New York: St. Martin's Press, 1983.

White, Theodore H. *The Making of the President 1960*. New York: Atheneum, 1961.

———*The Making of the President 1964*. New York: Atheneum, 1965.

———*The Making of the President 1968*. New York: Atheneum, 1969.

———*The Making of the President 1972*. New York: Atheneum, 1973.

———*America in Search of Itself*. New York: Harper & Row, 1982.

Whiting, Meredith, et al. *Campaign Finance Reform*. New York: The Conference Board, Inc., 1990.

Wilson, James Q. *The 1980 Election*. Lexington, Mass.: D.C. Heath, 1981.

Wolfinger, Raymond E., and Steven J. Rosenstone. *Who Votes?* New Haven, Conn.: Yale University Press, 1980.

*World Almanac and Book of Facts 1990*. New York: Pharos Books, 1989.

*World Almanac of U.S. Politics*, 1991–1993 ed. New York: Pharos Books, 1991.

# INDEX

Adams, John, 92, 118
Adams, John Quincy, 119, 129
Agnew, Spiro T., 29, 115
Alexander, Herbert, 31–32, 43
American Independent party, 12, 129
Anderson, John, 12, 86, 96
Armedaris, Alex, 80
Arthur, Chester A., 25, 72, 103, 12

Bayh, Birch, 96–97
Bentsen, Lloyd, 28, 72
Biden, Joseph, 28
Blacks, 18, 21, 30
Broder, David, 30, 74
Buchanan, James, 128
Buckley, James L., 11, 35
*Buckley* v. *Valeo,* 35–36, 47
Bull Moose party (Progressive party), 11, 129
Bundling, 44
Burr, Aaron, 92
Bush, George, 21, 25, 30, 42, 72, 73, 86, 92
Byrd, Harry F., 129

Calhoun, John C., 115
Campaign financing, 2, 31–49; current laws
    for, 123–25; Federal Election Campaign Act
    (FECA) of 1971 and, 2, 10–11; increase in,
    31–32; taxes and, 33, 48, 124–25
Cantor, Joseph E., 48
Carter, Jimmy, 25, 30, 43, 44, 59, 72, 77, 86, 100
Caucus/convention method of delegate selec-
    tion, 57–58, 60–61
Chisholm, Shirley, 30
Cleveland, Grover, 128
Closed primary, 56
Colorado, 56
Committee on Rules and Order of Business,
    Republican, 69
Committee work, conventions and, 67
Congress, U.S., 33, 85, 100, 101. *See also*

House of Representatives, U.S.; Senate,
    U.S.; House of Representatives, U.S.; Sen-
    ate, U.S. electoral college system reform
    and, 96–97 Federal Election Campaign Act
    (FECA) (1971) and, 32, 35, 36; voting rights
    and, 18–19
Congressional Campaign Committee, 10
Congressional Quarterly, Inc., 45
Connally, John, 42
Conservatives (Conservative party), 11
Constitution, U.S., 1, 6, 36, 106–8. *See also*
    *specific amendments*; Article II of, 106–7,
    109–12; electoral college system and,
    91–92; voters and, 14;
Conventions, 2, 3, 62–74, 119; president nom-
    inated at, 63, 70–71; start of, 69–70; vice
    president selection at, 63, 72–73
County committee, 8–9
Court of Appeals, U.S., 66
Credentials Committee, 68, 69
Cuomo, Mario, 28, 70

Debates, presidential, 85–87
Delegate selection, 3, 50–61; 1992, by state,
    52–55; evaluating, 60–61; methods, 50–58;
    caucus/convention, 57–58, 60–61; pri-
    maries, 51–58, 60–61; party reform and,
    58–60;
Democracy, Harwood study of, 16
Democratic National Committee, 7, 52, 56,
    58–59, 68
Democratic National Convention (1968 and
    1972), 58
Democratic party, 6, 11–12, 105, 120; cam-
    paign and, 80; conventions, 62–68, 70–73,
    119; delegate selection, 51–59; party
    reform, 58–59; in election of 1976, 27; in
    general election campaign, 77, 78, 85, 86;
    voter behavior and, 19–22
Democratic-Republicans, 6, 118

**135**

Direct delegate selection, 56
Direct presidential preference primary, 56
District of Columbia, 14, 17, 51, 66, 68, 92, 93, 96
Dole, Robert, 86
Dukakis, Michael, 21, 28, 42, 72, 92

Eisenhower, Dwight, 21, 27, 72
Election day, 97–100
Election of 1800, 92–94
Election of 1824, 93, 94
Election of 1844, 1852, 25
Election of 1852, 25
Election of 1860, 76
Election of 1868, 25
Election of 1876, 93
Election of 1884, 25
Election of 1888, 94
Election of 1912, third parties in, 11, 129
Election of 1924, third parties in, 11, 129
Election of 1948, 129
Election of 1952, 27
Election of 1960, 76, 85, 105, 129
Election of 1968, 7, 11, 12, 31, 25, 26, 100
Election of 1970, 11
Election of 1972, 14, 30, 94; campaign financing in, 31, 34, 40; conventions and, 65; ticket splitting in, 22
Election of 1976, 77, 92, 100; campaign financing in, 31, 41; debates, 85; preliminaries in, 26, 27, 30; third parties in, 12
Election of 1980, 12, 15, 21, 25, 59, 77–79, 96, 100–1; campaign financing in, 31–32, 40, 41, 42; conventions and, 70; debates, 86
Election of 1984, 27, 59; campaign, 78, 79; debates, 86; financing in, 41–42; conventions and, 70; voter behavior and, 21
Election of 1988; campaign, 79; financing, 40, 42; voter behavior, 21;
Election of 1992, 30; campaign, 62, 66, 79, 82; debates, 87; women and, 11, 82
Elections, 91–103; early projection of results, 100–1; electoral college system and, 91–97; proposals for change, 96–97; pros and cons of, 93–95; final stages of, 101–2; phases of, 2–4. See also specific phases; time frame of, 3; reporting the results of, 98–100
Electoral college system, 6, 91–97
Electoral votes, by state, 121–22
Electors, 107–8; "faithless," 94; selection of, 92
Equal-time provisions, 84–85, 124

Federal Communications Act, 124
Federal Communications Commission (FCC), 85
Federal Corrupt Practices Act (1925), 32
Federal Election Campaign Act (FECA) (1971), 2, 28, 32–48, 123; 1974 Amendments to, 33–35, 124; 1976 Amendments to, 36–37, 124; 1979 Amendments to, 38, 124; assessment of, 46–48; Buckley v. Valeo, 35–36, 47; campaign organization and, 76, 77; circumvention techniques and, 43–46; effects of, 42–46; political action committees and, 36–44
Federal Election Commission (FEC), 11, 34–38, 40, 123; criticism of, 46–47; functions of, 46
Federalists (Federalist party), 6, 118
Ferraro, Geraldine, 86
Fifteenth Amendment, 14, 116
Fillmore, Millard, 25
"Final Call to Convention," 66
First Amendment, 35, 66
Ford, Gerald, 25, 26, 30, 36, 86, 94
Fremont, John, 119

Garfield, James A., 128
Gender gap, 82
General election campaign, 3, 75–90; media in, 83–90; equal-time provisions, 84–85; news coverage, 83–84; presidential debates, 85–87; organization of, 76–77; strategy for, 78–81; tactics in, 81–82
Gerrymandering, 18
Goldwater, Barry, 100
Guam, 68

Harrison, Benjamin, 129
Hart, Gary, 28
Harwood Group, 16
Hayes, Rutherford B., 129
Heard, Alexander, 32
House of Representatives, U.S., 19, 22, 25, 103; campaign financing and, 37; electoral college system and, 92–95; Federal Election Campaign Act (FECA) (1971) and, 32, 36
Hughes, Sarah, 103
Humphrey, Hubert, 26, 27, 58
Hunt Commission (Commission on Presidential Nomination), 59

Idaho, 56
Inauguration, 102, 103
Independents, 12, 19–21
In-party preliminaries, 24–26
Iowa caucuses, 59

Jackson, Andrew, 115, 119
Jackson, Rev. Jesse, 28
Jefferson, Thomas, 92
Johnson, Andrew, 25
Johnson, Lyndon B., 21, 25, 100, . 103, 126

Kennedy, Edward, 127
Kennedy, John F., 72, 103, 105, 128, 129
Kennedy, Robert F., 26, 126
Kettering Foundation, 16

La Follette, Robert M., 11, 129
Lame-duck Amendment, 108
Lame duck president, 102
League of Women Voters Education Fund (LWVEF), 85–87
Lincoln, Abraham, 6, 76, 119, 128
Louisiana, 57
"Lowest-unit" rule, 124

McCarthy, Eugene, 12, 25, 26, 35
McGovern, George, 27, 65
McKinley, William, 126
Maine, 96
*Making of the President 1960* (White), 83
*Manchester Union Leader,* 30
Massachusetts, 45
Media. *See also* Television; in campaign, 83–90; in preliminaries, 29–30
Mondale, Walter, 21, 27, 80, 86
Monroe, James, 118
Mott, Stewart, 35
Multicandidate committees, 37, 48, 125
Muskie, Edmund, 30

National committee, 9–10
National Federation of Republican Women, 10
National Organization for Women (NOW), 11
National Voter Registration Act (Motor Voter Bill), (1991)18–19
New Hampshire primary, 45, 59, 87
Niemi, Richard G., 23
Nineteenth Amendment, 14, 116–17
Nixon, Richard M., 21, 29, 34, 58, 72, 76, 94, 115, 128, 129

Nomination process, presidential, 118–20
North Dakota, 17

Oath of office, 102, 103
Open primary, 55–56
Oregon, 119
Out-party preliminaries, 27–29

Parris, Judith N., 62
Party reform, 58–60
Permanent Organization Committee, Republican, 69
Platform Committee, Democratic, 68
Political action committees (PAC), 36–44, 124, 125; presidential, 43; separate, segregated fund type of, 39
*Political Action Committees: Their Evolution and Growth and Their Implications for the Political System* (Cantor), 48
Political parties, 2, 5–12. *See also specific parties*; electoral college system and, 92; other political groups and, 10–12; role of, 5–7; structure of, 7–10; county committee, 8–9; national committee, 9–10; precinct, 8; state committee, 9; voter behavior and, 19–22
Polk, James K., 128
Populists (Populist party), 11
Power, presidential, 1–2
Precinct, 8
Preliminaries, 24–30; in-party, 24–26; media in, 29–30; out-party, 27–29
President, U.S., nomination of, 63, 70–71; office of, 109–15; duties and powers, 111–12; oath of office, 110; qualifications, 109; remuneration, 110–11; succession, 112–14; term, 109–10; power of, 1–2; protection of candidates for, 126–27
Presidential Election Campaign Fund, 33, 125
Presidential Succession Act (1947), 113–14
Primaries, 51–58, 87, 119–20; evaluation of, 60–61; New Hampshire, 45; terminology for, 55–57
Progressives (Progressive party) (Bull Moose party), 11, 129
Proportional, definition of, 56
Puerto Rico, 51, 68

Quayle, Dan, 72, 73

Radio, advertising on, 32–33, 88–90
Reagan, Ronald, 21, 25, 42, 44, 72, 73, 77, 78, 86, 94, 100, 124–25

Realignment, 7, 12

Reeves, Richard, 80

Registration, voter, 17

Remuneration, presidential, 110–11

Republican National Committee, 52, 60

Republican party, 11–12, 105, 120; campaign and, 80; conventions, 62, 63, 66, 68–73, 119; delegate selection and, 51–56, 59–60; party reform, 59–60; in general election campaign, 76–78, 85, 86–87; origins of, 6; voter behavior and, 19–22

Resolutions Committee, Republican, 69

Results, election; early projection of, 100–1; reporting of, 98–100

Revenue Act (1971), 33, 48

Ripon Society, 66

Robertson, Marion G. (Pat), 42

Rockefeller, Nelson A., 26

Roosevelt, Franklin, 72, 73

Roosevelt, Theodore, 11, 120, 129

Rules Committee, Democratic, 68

Schlesinger, Arthur Jr., 73

Senate, U.S., 19, 22, 25, 27, 93, 95, 97; campaign financing and, 37; Federal Election Campaign Act (FECA) (1971) and, 32, 36

Senate Campaign Committee, 10

Seventeenth Amendment, 14, 116

South Dakota, 56

Stanley, Harold W., 23

State(s). *See also specific states;* delegate selection by, 52–55; electoral votes by, 121–22; size of, electoral college system and, 94

State committee, 9

States' Rights party (Dixiecrat), 129

Stevenson, Adlai, 72

Supreme Court, U.S., 17, 102; *Buckley* v. *Valeo,* 35–36, 47; campaign financing and, 37; one-person-one-vote ruling and, 96; voting rights and, 18

Taft, William, 120

Taxes, campaign financing and, 33, 48, 124–25

Taylor, Zachary, 128

Television; campaigns and, 84–90; candidate advertising, 32–33, 80, 88–90; conventions and, 73–74; election coverage on, 98–100

Tennessee, 57

Term of office, presidential, 109–10

Texas, 57

Third parties, 11–12, 96, 129

*Thornburg* v. *Gingles,* 18

Thurmond, J. Strom, 129

Truman, Harry S, 128

Twelfth Amendment, 92–93, 107–8

Twentieth Amendment, 103, 108, 110

Twenty-fourth Amendment, 14, 17, 117

Twenty-second Amendment, 25, 110

Twenty-sixth Amendment, 117

Twenty-third Amendment, 14, 92

Two-party system, 6–7

Twenty-third Amendment, 117

Tyler, John, 25

Utah, 56

Vacancies in the vice presidency, 114–15

Van Buren, Martin, 119

Vice president; electoral college system and, 92–93; selection of, 63, 72–73; vacancies in, 114–15;

Virgin Islands, 68

*Vital Statistics on American Politics* (Stanley and Niemi), 23

Voters, 13–23; choices of, 3–4; expansion of, 13–14, 116–17

Voting Rights Act (1965), 17–18

Voting Rights Act (1970), 18

Voting Rights Act (1975), 18

Voting Rights Act (1982), 18

Wallace, George C., 12, 29, 94, 96, 129

Washington, DC, 14, 17, 51, 66, 68, 92, 93, 96

Washington state, 57

Washington, George, 118

*Washington Post,* 30

Watergate investigations, 33–34

Whigs (Whig party), 6, 119

White, Theodore H., 30, 83

*White* v. *Regester,* 18

Wilson, Woodrow, 128

Winner-take-all system, 56, 94, 95

Wirt, William, 119

Young Democrats, 10